Between the Heartbeats

Between the Heartbeats

POETRY & PROSE BY NURSES

Edited by CORTNEY DAVIS & JUDY SCHAEFER

UNIVERSITY OF IOWA PRESS ♈ *Iowa City*

University of Iowa Press, Iowa City 52242

Copyright © 1995 by the University of Iowa Press

All rights reserved

Printed in the United States of America

Design by Richard Hendel

Printed on acid-free paper

Library of Congress Cataloging-in-Publication Data

Between the heartbeats: poetry and prose by nurses / edited by
Cortney Davis and Judy Schaefer.

p.   cm.

ISBN 0-87745-516-3, ISBN 0-87745-517-1 (paper)

1. Nurses' writings, American.   2. Nurse and patient — Literary
collections.   3. American literature — 20th century.   4. Nursing —
Literary collections.   5. Nurses — Literary collections.   I. Davis,
Cortney, 1945– .   II. Schaefer, Judy, 1944–

PS508.N87B48   1995

810.8'092613—dc20   95-30297

                                                              CIP

01   00   99   98   97   96   95   c   5   4   3   2   1

01   00   99   98   97   P   5   4   3

CONTENTS

Foreword

JOANNE TRAUTMANN BANKS

The truth is that when we are sick, very sick, it is often the nurse who is closest to our bodies, minds, and souls. She is closer than today's doctor, who is in and out too fast; closer than the hospital chaplain, who doesn't stick around for the telling physical details; sometimes closer, even, than the family, who can't face all the secrets that illness uncovers. In fact, Nurse (her *name*, as one of the poems in this anthology has it) is present at a great many human crises, whether they take place at hospitals, clinics, or homes.

So why don't we know what the nurse thinks about all this intimacy? Where are the records that address our peculiar vulnerability? Certainly, they are not in nursing textbooks, where "biopsychosocial" approaches lump us all together like so much data or scatter our idiosyncrasies among artificial case histories. Nor are the records of nurse-patient intimacy found in the standard medical chart, where a nurse's hastily written phrases— "patient in tears" or "attempted to reassure him"—are only an expedient shorthand. Nurses' voices are not clearly heard in medical novels, films, and television, where, as in life, doctors dominate.

Happily, in this book literary nurses are at last in charge. Their voices, speaking sometimes in poetry, sometimes in prose, have never before been heard in such numbers. And what a remarkable chorus they make! It's as if all those scurrying figures in white shoes have been allowed to slow down long enough to complete their songs and stories.

Now we can learn what some of our caregivers were thinking while they were taking our vital signs. Generally, overwhelmingly, it's what we hoped for. Nurses, this book tells us, listen to our trivial talk about dogs and cars and pot roasts, and recognize that we are trying hard to stitch together a life. They realize that all the while we are indirectly talking about death. Nurses respect us even when we are comatose. They cheer us when we survive an illness. When we don't, they miss us in concrete, individual terms. They admit that they are only temporarily vertical, and they often identify with their horizontal patients.

But the book also confirms our fears. Nurses, it turns out, see our unlovely bodies in horrific detail. They inhale our stench. They roll their eyes at each other to indicate that we don't know what we're talking about. Behind the nurses' station they change us into nicknames to give them control and to pass the time—"Jabba the Hut" because one of us is obese, "Mick Jagger" because another has flapping lips.

And yet nurses are vulnerable too. Indeed, part of the impact of this book derives from the writers' harsh honesty about their own limits and the limits of their profession. Psychologically, these are life-and-death limits, and the possibility of running smack into them exists every time a nurse goes to work. For instance, the temptation to treat patients mechanistically is very nearly universal in the profession. Based on the evidence of *Between the Heartbeats*, mechanistic routine, and the distancing it causes, is at least as dangerous to nurses as to patients. After all, in Sarah Collings' story "Hospital Course," "Mick Jagger" isn't directly hurt by being reduced behind his back to flapping lips. He doesn't die from it. But when Jagg does die from another cause, the nurse who nicknamed him dies a little herself. She is not free to scream "like the families do"—that is, like living, involved people do—but instead falls back into what she sees as "comfortable" professional language to describe his collapse—"an unmonitored arrest, patient noncompliant." Such language gets her through. It is even proper in the context, but at what cost to her sense of self?

A second kind of limit that runs through these pieces is nurses' powerlessness in the face of disease, suffering, and, especially, death. Doctors write about powerlessness too, but with nurses there is, I want to say, even more poignancy. I suppose that doctors get from their training the idea that they and death are, if not equals—no one is death's equal—at least its powerful adversaries. Doctors, armed with drugs and knives, are told that they should seek a cure. They should lead the charge. Nurses, armed with thermometers and dressings, are told to assist, to comfort, to seek optimal functioning for their patients. In other words, nurses are not licensed to use full force in the battle with disease. As the nurse says of the lovely, dying child in Jeanne Bryner's poem "Blue Lace Stockings," "I try to buy time with only coffee money / in my pocket." All the same, they are on the front line, these nurses, so their inevitable losses are particularly moving. "Since I can offer you nothing else," writes the nurse in Amy Haddad's "Dehiscence," "I clean you up."

Given this passive despair, it is understandable that sometimes nurses want to burst out of professional limits. For instance, the young neonatal nurse in Belle Waring's "Euthanasia" decides that she will no longer stand by and watch the tiny creature in her care being used by the residents "for IV practice." But the poem's more experienced nurse knows that questions about suffering are never so easily answered. So, instead of arguing with her young coworker, she shoulders the ambiguities of her profession and escapes outside for a smoke.

In spite of the heavy presence of such pain in these pages, the book is not in the least hard to bear. For one thing, medical horrors are not offered as merely sensational and nothing more. There is no "cult of suffering," in Theodore Deppe's phrase, or much "love of storms," as he says in another poem, for their own sake. In fact, the effect of the human storms is lessened by the detail with which they are presented. That is, by looking unsentimentally at suffering, these nurse-writers are performing an act of loving care. Furthermore, there is a surprising variety in the collection, and that too eases the reader's path among the stricken patients. There are in-patients, out-patients, and home patients of mixed social classes. Their attendants are young and old, female and, increasingly, male. Some of the nurses are dispassionately efficient. Others wickedly admit to the joys of voyeurism. The poems are nicely varied as to line and diction, and the prose, like many of the narratives written by doctors, runs along that thin and exciting line between fiction and essay. Just when the present is too much with us, the editors take us to the past for reminiscences of Vietnam or nursing school. There is a good deal of welcome charm in these memoirs of restrictive old nursing schools, all of which sound to me like slightly mad convents.

Finally, I want to predict the shocks that await readers of this book, even, I would guess, the old hands at suffering—other clinicians, for instance, or people living with chronic illness. I, for one, have for twenty-five years been with the same sorts of people, witnessed the same sorts of events, that these nurse-writers evoke. At least, I thought I'd been there. Every so often my reaction to one of the pieces has been that astonishment, composed equally of aesthetic and moral elements, which slices open the soul. I could list those moments, but of course other readers must feel themselves to be completely free and susceptible. I would, however, like to take away the hyphen from those unnamed nurse-writers who shocked me. Call them simply writers who happen to have unusual access to us.

Nighthawks

CAROLYN BARBIER *Albuquerque, New Mexico*

I know I'm in a hospital. I know it's serious and I should be scared. I cannot quite remember what has happened. I feel more excited than alarmed. I feel the adrenaline of the moment pushing me.

A tube presses my tongue flat on the floor of my mouth, and it bulges against my teeth. The pipe reaches down my throat. It branches out of my mouth against one corner, pulling my lips down on that side. A young woman secures the tube with tape across my upper lip. I want to fix it like a bulky fold of sock in my shoe. When she's finished, she smiles, cocks her head, and pats the tape—her package wrapped, the bow in place. "You're going to be just fine," she says. I want to tell her how I'm sure she's right.

I want to tell all these people I will work with them. I smile and nod, but they don't notice. Occasionally, they look over at me and tell me something they're about to do to me and how it will feel. They speak normally to one another, but when they turn to me, they speak loudly and articulate very distinctly. They call me Hon or say OK as a question.

Of course it's OK. You go right ahead with what you're doing.

I want to cooperate with them, to show them I'm part of the team. The room is bright, all the lights are on, but the window is dark. It is night.

* * *

I wake up inside my eyelids. I listen. No voices now except for a woman in the distance. Her tone is kind but businesslike, and I imagine her assisting a phone customer with an order for take-out food.

For a moment I think I hear waves. But the whooshing is too constant and marked regularly by a loud pop. I realize these sounds match my own tense breathing. I can't relax. I have to keep time.

I remember lying next to my mother as a child. She is sleeping. I try to match my breathing to hers. Her breaths are longer than mine. I concentrate. I push the air out slowly. The emptiness in my lungs stings. I wait for her to inhale.

Years later, I would lie awake next to Joe as he slept. I resisted, but the old childhood habit would creep back until I noticed I was breathing faster than I liked to keep up with him. I switched just short of full and just short of empty. I would catch myself working hard to keep his rhythm and had to move away from him to the other side of the bed.

Now, in this narrow bed, I have no choice. I try, but I can't move. A machine with a rhythm only partially related to my own is breathing for me whether I want it to or not. It blasts air into my lungs before I have a chance to empty them completely. I hear it switch, loud and hard. I try to match it. I wait for it. I ache inside with desire for air. I try to be ready, but it startles me. It jams air into me.

I open my eyes. The room was bright before. Now it is like a bedroom with a pale reading light. The hall beams a reflection on the shiny floor. A young man sits in the doorway, using a bedside table as a writing desk. He sips from a mug that says, "You want it when?" His baggy green scrubs accentuate the sinew and muscles of his bare arms and neck. I imagine touching his firm skin. He writes and glances up and writes more. He doesn't glance at me but rather past me. I picture a large scoreboard on the wall above me. He sees something which concerns him and moves toward me, adjusts something behind me, and sits to write more.

I try to signal him. I move my fingers and wave—a polite, country-road kind of wave. The effort surprises me. He doesn't see me, so I decide to flag him down by waving my arms. I discover my arms are too weak. My hands are tied to the bed. Bound softly with fabric straps in wide loops. I must have done something earlier to deserve being tied now. I hang on to this rationalization to quiet the panic.

* * *

"Ms. Paige . . . can you hear me?"

I open my eyes. The room is light now. Light everywhere. Daylight.

A man in his early fifties stands next to my bed. "I'm Dr. Ruskin." He holds a folder open, resting it on the side rail above my face. He looks from the equipment behind me, down at his papers and the men and women gathered around. He speaks about me.

He looks into my face when he speaks to me.

Flecks of color in his tie pick up the blue of his shirt. His graying blond hair is waved carefully in place. I envision a woman's long fingers with lacquered nails giving it shape. He must have shaved only five minutes ago. His discreet clean scent refreshes me in this room so full of strong odors.

"You were very lucky, young lady. Those Coast Guard guys got you out of the water just in time."

The water. I remember the storm. I had to get off the water.

The doctor talks on in the easy tones of a salesman showing a new line of designer shoes. I am distracted by the ragamuffin band of his followers. Some have red eyes. Some look two or three days past bathing. One has buttoned his shirt in the wrong buttonholes. Another has lipstick smeared past the perimeter of her lips.

I hear Dr. Ruskin's voice summing up, ". . . so, your job is to get through this present crisis. After that, we'll begin to discuss the possibilities for the future. But, let's not worry about that now. You're going to be just fine." He smiles, but none of his students smile. Each face in the room is trained on mine. What do all these people know about me?

After they leave, I try to remember what he said. I try to relax. I try to shut off my mind. What possibilities for the future?

* * *

The light is bright in the room and the noise in the hallway is constant. I hear hard footsteps coming closer, like leather pumps, not the comfortable rubberized soles worn by the people who work here. I hear the even teaching voice of a nurse moving closer with the click of the pumps. My shoulders stiffen.

The sound of the heels stops outside my door but the voice continues, ". . . her face is quite swollen. Prepare yourself because she won't look like Margaret to you. She can't talk and can only feel and move her hands a little. But remember, she's fully conscious and can hear and communicate. If you'll try to be patient."

My mother walks in the door wearing a charcoal gray skirt and lighter gray sweater. Her turquoise scarf and silver hair lift the monochrome. She smiles as though caught in an embarrassing moment of recognizing a face but not remembering the name. She stands in the doorway, giving herself a moment to adjust.

"Margaret . . . sweetheart, I'm so glad to see you." She crosses to the bedside. "I just got here and took a taxi right over from the airport." She takes my hand and considers it. "You look. . . ." She closes her eyes and bends down to kiss my cheek. Her face has softened when she moves back to look at me again, and she smiles. "It's so good to see you. I couldn't wait to get here. I was desperate to see . . . for myself."

My mother is the first person who knew me before the accident to see me now. I had not looked in a mirror until she walked in the door.

* * *

I can tell time by the level of light in the room. I know there is a clock on the wall to my left but I can't turn far enough to see it. I know it's there because a nurse will occasionally glance toward it and tell me what time it is. I no longer tell time by my usual six A.M. shower, round of lectures and appointments in my office, or a relaxing martini before dinner.

Now, when I am being bathed, I know it is sometime around three in the morning. It is about five in the morning when my blood is drawn. If it's daylight outside and my blood is drawn, I know my numbers are wrong. A new nurse comes on duty and I know it is seven in the evening if it's dark outside the window, seven in the morning if it's light. There are never any meals.

I tell myself every few minutes, you can do this.

* * *

I wonder what floor of the hospital I am on. The large window gives me a view of the building next door. A view of one brown brick wall. The building must be very tall because I can't see the sky above it. I try to remember the layout of this part of the city and what building it is. Light changes the color of the bricks and they entertain me. When they are dark, an organic chocolate brown, I assume it is cloudy outside. I can't see the sun, but it shines in the flecks of mica in the brick. Once, I was thrilled to see the bricks sparkling but also dappled with deep chocolate as raindrops fell.

I think of my studio. My hands yearn to mold clay, to capture the stippled quality of the brick, and to glaze it with flecked brown.

I can see the window, the door into the hallway, and the supply cabinet on the far wall of the room. Each person who works over me makes trip after trip to the cabinet and back. At one time I began counting the trips required to complete one procedure. My intention was to count, then average them. I lost count somewhere.

Oftentimes, the cabinet door hangs open with a half-folded sheet tumbling out toward the floor. I lie here imagining myself folding the sheet. Putting it back on the shelf. When I try to ask the nurse to close the door with small pointing motions toward it, she always tries to guess what I want inside. The guessing frustrates both of us.

The nurses and doctors laugh and joke in the hall right up to the threshold of my room, where they suddenly become solemn and professional. I imagine a transformation shield stands in the doorway. I want to ask them to bring their funny stories into my room with them. I hope there is light in my eyes when they look at me, but I can't tell.

* * *

It is dark. I can tell dark and light through my eyelids. I can hear the nighthawks calling as they dart between the buildings, snatching insects from the air. Their cry is loud and nasal, an unattractive buzz. And yet, it is wild and alluring.

The first two years I lived in this city, I loved the sound but never knew what bird made it. I heard it late at night while driving home from dinner with friends. I knew it was not safe to drive alone with all the windows rolled down, but the city was quiet, the air was cool, and the streets almost empty. I drove fast to feel my hair blown across my face. At that hour, the city belonged to me. It didn't threaten me with all its unknown. It belonged to the nighthawks, and they flew, freewheeling in the air between the buildings.

I feel that exhilaration now, in this bed, when I hear them call outside. I want to reach over and push the window open, to feel the air on my face.

* * *

I am lying on my side, propped by pillows. I am facing the window and the brown bricks beyond it. The dull lack of color in the wall tells me it is just before dawn. I have been bathed, and for just this one moment, I feel neat between my cool clean sheets. Tonight, Angela is my nurse. She takes care of me often. When I first saw the name on her badge, I was sure it had to be a joke, a nurse called "angel." We have become accustomed to one another, and I feel at ease when she walks into my room.

Angela comes in now and I hear her behind me. "Oh, no, Margaret, not again." I notice the familiar sweet concentrated smell and immediately feel ashamed. She keeps assuring me it will only take a moment to clean up, that everything's just fine. I see the way she will not look at me. I see the tears she can't wipe away because her gloves are smeared dark brown.

It's not just fine, Angela.

She tells me not to pay any attention to her—it has been a tough night and she's ready to go home.

Later, I see her walking down the hall with her coat over her arm. She usually says good-bye to me before she leaves. She wants to get away from here as fast as she can. So do I.

* * *

The room is barely light, but Dr. Ruskin's arrival with his colleagues means it is eight in the morning. I assume the sky is cloudy, and the spatters on the window please me when they begin.

The rain started. My hands were wet. The wind ripped at the mainsail and the waves tore the rudder in my grip.

"We haven't been able to wean you off the ventilator, Margaret, and you can't breathe on your own. It looks like you're going to be on the machine a long time, and the tube's been in your mouth for three weeks now. Way, way too long." He speaks to me in a light tone, but when he asks one of the students for an interpretation of my numbers, his voice deepens and his wording is complex.

"So, we're going to make a hole in your throat for the breathing tube. You'll be much more comfortable this way. We'll all try to read your lips so you can complain about the way we're treating you."

I expect him to take a knife out of his pocket and cut my throat. I won't complain, I promise. He laughs and pats my hand. Several of the students smile on their way out the door.

I'm confused. Then I realize they will take me to the operating room and put me to sleep.

Wean. A child learning to feed herself after a life of drinking only from her mother's breast. An addict giving up a beloved drug slowly, to make the pain of withdrawal more tolerable.

I wait for the machine-driven blast of air. I need it. I am relieved when it enters me.

* * *

"Margaret? Wake up, honey. It's me, it's your momma."

I open my eyes to the brightness of the room and my mother's smile. She wears deep brown slacks and a blue knit blouse that looks soft to the touch.

"Good morning, sweetheart. You look all nice and clean and ready for a new day. It's a beautiful day, too. Look, the sun's shining bright, not a cloud in the sky." She goes to the window and cranes her head upward near the glass. As she turns back to me she looks stricken, wishing she'd said something different. I smile, but the tube pulls one side of my mouth down. I want to make her comfortable. "Well, at least it's nice and bright in here." She pulls a chair up to the side of the bed.

"I've been busy this morning. Let's see. . . . I made a couple phone calls. I called Lori, of course. We decided to rent one hotel room nearby. She said she'd make reservations to come down right away.

Stop.

"She has to shop around a little to get the best fare, and I said I'd help her out with that, so she'll be here as soon as she can. Before you know it. And with a room nearby, one of us can be here with you and the other can get some rest."

Stop.

"Your house is just too far away to keep shuttling back and forth like I've been doing for the last week. I think it'll work out just fine."

Stop. Please. I don't know what you're saying.

"And, honey, I called Joe."

Stop. Stop and explain. I can only roll my eyes and feel silly doing it.

"I know. It felt a little awkward calling him, I can tell you that. He was terribly upset, but he was glad I called."

Stop.

"I think he still misses you. Did I do the right thing, honey?"

I just stare at her.

"I thought he at least deserved to know about the accident and what a rough time you've had bouncing back." She stops a moment and looks at me. "I feel so clumsy sitting here talking to you like this. Tomorrow after the surgery you can tell me all about it. I'll learn to lip read, I promise. Anyway, Joe said to give you his best and to let him know if there was anything he could do."

I don't need anything Joe could do.

"I think maybe he feels a little guilty. He was the one who got you interested in the damn boat."

That's true, but he hated my love for it.

She pulls her lips in over her teeth and bites them until they are white edges. "He said to tell you he still loves you."

Don't.

She stands and moves to the window, then turns to me the way she would with a great new idea. "Margaret, you've got to be strong, you know. Dr. Ruskin says we've got to get your lungs cleared out or they'll scar even more. And then you'll never breathe on your own again. You don't want that, do you, sweetie?"

And if you don't wipe that ugly look off your face, young lady, it's going to freeze that way.

"He says when you're better, they can start therapy to help you use your arms some. You've got to come out of this. You've got to fight."

I was fighting to hold the rudder. My hands were wet.

"You have all these folks pulling for you, people who care about you."

I was reaching for the halyard to reef the mainsail.

She laughs. Her hands are in fists. "See, I almost forgot. Dr. Jaynes calls almost everyday, even though he knows you won't be back to the university."

Stop.

"He just wants to check on you. He says to tell you how very much you'll be missed. Do you understand me, Hon?"

No, I don't understand. I want my studio. I want my art. I want my students.

"What, honey? What are you trying to say?"

I reached for the halyard and the rudder pulled out of my hands. Then it slammed back into my side. The boat pitched.

"Now just relax. Everything's going to be just fine." She looks over my head and behind me. People often look at the equipment there when talking to me is difficult. "Do you want me to get the nurses? Are you OK? I just don't know how to communicate with you right now."

She turns to the window and I see her hand go to her eye, but when she shifts back toward me she is defiantly perky. "You listen to me. You pull yourself out of this little crisis and we'll fly you back to Denver in a special plane. You know, ever since your Daddy died I've been so lonesome. Then you left Joe and I started thinking. It'd be fun for both of us to live together."

Stop.

"Now we have our chance. This way I can take care of you. I know you like your independence, but you're still my little girl. You need me now."

Stop.

"I know that's not the right thing to say, but it's true. We can get one of those nurses who come right to the house. We'll be good company for each other. I know I could use some company. I can make it up to you for always being too busy. I remember times when I'd buy you a new dress and wouldn't get it hemmed before you grew out of it. After all these years, I wish I could've balanced things out better. What do you think?" She leans forward and takes my hand. "I know. We don't have to decide anything right now. You rest and I'll just sit here with you for a while."

She pulls her knitting out of her bag and starts to work. I watch her steady hands hold the needles and make quick repetitive movements, wrapping the yarn around again and again. She notices me watching her and smiles at me.

I think of being in the same room with her for days on end, listening to her. Unable to say a word. The way it used to feel years and years ago.

I remember the joy I felt living alone after ten years of marriage to Joe. Deciding when I would eat, working in my studio as late as I wanted, going for days without turning on the television. I liked sailing more than he did. The boat allowed me to escape his constant evaluation of me. On the water I was free of his critique. When I first left, I thought I felt no grief and would never cry.

Then, I walked into the studio and accidentally shut the door on the tips of my fingers. I howled with pain and knelt down over my stool and held myself while I wept. All the pain and grief I felt collected there in my fingertips. I knew it was right to finally feel my loss through the part of me I used to touch the world, to mold clay.

I try to feel my fingers now. I know they are there, but they are unavailable. I don't recognize them. My body is like a concealed identity on TV. The face is camouflaged by flashing colored squares, but occasionally the outline of the jaw or the hair bleeds out over the edge.

I think of living with Momma, with her as my hands and eyes and speech. Her interpretation of the world, her evaluations and critique. Reclaimed by the womb.

I want to hold a book, to read, and to turn the pages myself.

* * *

Someone is in the room with me. Someone is sitting by the bed. I can hear the squeaky suck of chewing gum and the rough rub of denim as legs in blue jeans are crossed. I can hear the pages of a book flip up at the corner and slide slowly through fingers as it is turned over. I decide to open my eyes. It used to be an automatic movement.

Lori sits in an orange molded-plastic chair. Her jeans are designer, but her blouse is rumpled. She wears her long blonde hair swept back from her face, and her makeup is perfect. I want to throw my arms around her, to tell her how happy I am to see her. Or, at least, to scream at her. Her fingers slide down the page of the book in her hand. She slowly turns her head to the left as she turns the page and glances at me in passing.

"Hey, cutey! We were wondering when you were going to check back in." She unfolds her tall body, unloads her book, and comes over to me. She leans down to hug me. Her perfume feels like a dull blade in my nostrils. "Damn, it's good to see you in there. They did the surgery three days ago. I guess you needed some time to sleep it off."

Sleep is the great escape, Lori. You know that.

She strokes my forehead and holds my hand. I am so used to the probing intimate touch of strangers, the sweetness of this touch from a friend stuns me. I miss it so much it hurts.

My nurse enters the room to tend my tubes and bottles and adjust my equipment. Lori proudly presents me in my newly conscious state, as though it were something she and I accomplished together. The nurse seems very pleased to see me and says they've all been worried about me. She introduces herself as Debbie to Lori. "Dora told me all about you—how you and Margaret have been best friends for years and all."

It's odd to hear my mother referred to as Dora. The conversation we had. Not a conversation. When? Dora, in her brown slacks and blue blouse, telling me how she's picked up my life where I left off. Lori, get me out of here.

"Well, I couldn't stay away, could I?" Lori says. "Margaret and I have been best friends for almost twenty years."

"Boy, that's a long time." Debbie hardly looks twenty herself.

"We've been through everything together. Every new style, every new project, and every new man. I bet if you added up all the husbands and boyfriends and lovers we've had between us and laid them end to end, they'd stretch for at least three city blocks."

She squeezes my hand harder, and I look to the nurse to check her reaction. Lori follows and sees the younger woman's wide eyes and solid plaster smile. I want her to stop this performance, but she rushes on.

"And, what do we have left after all that? Just each other." She looks down at me. "I know I sure couldn't ask for anything more." Lori grins the same lewd way she did when we were twenty-two and comparing fish stories about our current men.

Don't, Lori.

"To tell the truth, I wouldn't mind getting laid a little more often." Debbie shares Lori's laugh, but her hand covers her mouth and her face is down. The laugh in my chest battles with the machine-driven burst of air and loses to a cough. I see Debbie pat my foot on her way out but cannot feel it.

Lori shakes her head. "Well, I guess I really impressed her, didn't I? I always say the stupidest things when I'm nervous."

Talk to me, Lori. I'm scared.

She walks over to the window and says, "They sure gave you a crappy view." Her shirt is taut across her hunched shoulders, her fingernail in her mouth.

Talk to me, Lori. Tell me why you're so scared.

"Well, I promise you one thing, girl." She turns around to me and smiles. "When you get out of here, I'm coming down for that visit you keep asking me to make."

No. Get me out of here now.

"What is it, Marg? You don't want me to come?"

Yes. You're the only one who can get me out of here.

"It'd be great. You always make me so much more adventurous. We'd have a great time. What are you trying to say? I know, I've been a real poop. You must be totally disgusted with me. I don't know why I've been putting it off so long. Life just never lets up with these little lessons, like you always say."

What little lessons? Like make hay while the sun shines? Or maybe, you don't miss your water till your well runs dry?

I am shaking my head as far to each side as I can. My neck hurts as if hands are around it squeezing tight. My mouth is dry and feels full of my tongue without the tube to hold it flat. I begin to mouth the words. NO. NO. OFF. OFF.

* * *

To look at the bowl sitting on the table is like looking at a photograph of me. Me before. Its surface is smooth and crimson and as the lip curves inward at the mouth, the creamy underglaze shines through. I have always refused to sell it, no matter what the offer. I kept it, so I could see my own ability to create. Now it doesn't matter.

Angela is washing my legs. I can see her lift each foot and rotate it, lift each leg and bend it at the knee. "Gotta keep those joints moving," she says. She spreads lotion on my legs. "Sorry my hands are cold, Margaret." She looks at me, narrowing her eyes. "God, that was a stupid thing for me to say." I can feel a cool pressure when she holds my hand and looks me in the face.

"So, Dora brought this bowl in. I think she wanted to make you feel better."

Angela's fingers run along the curving lip of the bowl with the same tenderness I can see when she touches my legs. "You must be really good. I mean, I don't know anything about art, but this is wonderful."

Angela who is full of wonder.

She holds the bowl up toward the light and touches the glaze. She watches me while she says, "I don't know, I guess I might be all wet, but it just seems a little teensy bit mean to me, to bring this." She puts the bowl down. "But I'm sure her intentions are good."

Take it. I mouth the words slowly. I want you to have the bowl, Angela.

"Here, let me roll you over so I can do your back."

I shake my head no. Take it.

She resists. She says she can't. She says it would be unprofessional. Then, "Do you really mean it? You really, really want me to?"

She's behind me. I can hear the water splash lightly and drip off the washcloth as she lathers soap. I see her bend while she washes my back. The sound of the wet cloth and slippery soap almost convinces me I can feel it.

"Lori stopped me when I came on tonight. She's really shook. I guess she's scared, but I know she wants what's best for you, Margaret. I'm just going to clean down here between your legs. You have to be sure, really sure. Lori will stand up for you, and I will too. Here, let's roll you back and I'll fix your hair. It's getting long. Lori says she thinks you want the ventilator taken off."

* * *

The window is dark and the movement in the hallway outside my door has slowed. It's evening. My friend, my doctor of refreshing smells, is leaning against the doorway of my room.

I hear my mother's voice demanding, "Don't I have any say-so in this?"

"Yes, as next of kin you certainly do. But ultimately it is Margaret's decision," he explains, leaning down to her.

"I'm trying to understand. Every inch of me is her mother and wants to keep her alive. I want her alive, don't you understand?"

"I understand. I'm a physician. I want to keep her alive."

I can see Lori, tall and blonde, pacing just beyond.

"She's all I have left in the world."

Dr. Ruskin stands straight. "The chances of her ever breathing on her own again are very remote. She thought all this through when she signed a living will years ago." He glances back toward me and notices me watching, listening. "It's her decision." He reaches inside the room and pulls the door closed.

* * *

I hear Dr. Ruskin's quiet shoes creak in the hallway. His hair is still in a perfect finger wave and his shave is close, but now he wears the same exhausted look as his ragamuffin compatriots. Angela is his partner now. He asks whether I'm sure I understand. I hope he understands. He explains about the sedative and the removal of the breathing tube.

Angela holds my hand, and this time does not hide her wet eyes. Lori holds my other hand, her body erect, elegant in her courage. When the tube slides out, my throat closes and I feel I will choke. My body insists I breathe, but I cannot. I remember the water over my face becoming deeper and deeper. My lungs curse me, and for a moment I doubt I can stand the pain. Then I hear the nighthawks. They call to me as they fly.

The Color of Protocol

JEANNE BEALL *Lewiston, Idaho*

It's difficult to reconstruct
just how we were or how it was
in '68, that summer, still days
bathed in honeysuckle, sweltery damp
clothes a second skin, on our shoulders
silver bars that gleamed even
when the sun didn't shine.
Bits and pieces. Hail to the Chief,
each soldier's song, salutes
under skies the color of protocol.
Summer camp, the medical bus,
crisp blue members of the 22nd
squadron, we rode the bus past barracks,
innocence, and midnight;
necessary rumble of wheels on asphalt fields,
airstrip-airlift, bilious belly
kissing its cargo home.
The sickest hung like soldered sloths,
suspended berths in webs of tubes
and cotton, pumps and drainage,
borrowed space from tanks and jeeps,
bodies bent and broken by war.
Telescopic vision, close-up of loss:
flesh like mine peppered by shrapnel,
legs blown apart, tripped by mines,
and minds severed from their bodies.
Windowed souls and empty orbits,
halves of faces, excavated melons, vacant.
No one lives there anymore.
A prisoner of war who looks like my brother,
three long years, home from Cambodia,
his hands outstretched, molded like a rice bowl,
begs canned peaches and a T-bone.

Angel from Pratt Street

JEANNE BEALL *Lewiston, Idaho*

Knees worn through like any other kid's,
he lay on the gurney, pants high-water
to ankles that had no feet.
Just that morning he was eight,
playing with matches
in a hand tenuous as ash.
Cutting down the seams, I couldn't tell
his color — black and charred, maroon
ribbons of muscle under skin
peeled down like onions.
For weeks he lay in quiet ruin,
boy in an old man,
mummy-wrapped in bandages
neon in their whiteness.

I like to think he soared that night
beyond the ceilinged heavens of St. Luke's,
beyond St. Louis, Missouri, this world,
his narcoleptic chamber broken
by a solo unwinged flight
ethereal and actual as air.
That night he rose
through tattered light off crystal tubes
like nets around his knees.
Feathered remnants, clouds of gauze
swirled, then spiraled down.
From across the room, I saw him
suspended in an ornamental instant,
clear and fragile, falling
through the ever-lucid air
beyond my reach, little boy,
solitary angel of glass.

Why Not Me?

JANET BERNICHON *Shirley, New York*

I rolled my eyes and said in a stage whisper,
"His mother wants everything done."
Tommy's thin ice body barely wrinkled the sheets—
chest caved in, percolator breaths,
sunken eyes, mouth slack exposing teeth.
Hello, Mr. Death, I thought,
eyes blank
as I passed his mother.

I didn't like him.
He had track marks on his arms and ankles,
he had shattered his mother like fine porcelain on a dirty road.
He was my son's age and was dying,

separated from us by a glass partition
and the modern medical miracle—
life support. A respirator
marked time in the slow wait.
His mother had her back to me
in her vigil. She enclosed his hand,
the flesh of her flesh, in hers
as if the tight hold
could keep him from slipping away.
She said, "Why, Tommy, why you?"

In the window, my reflection
stood within this tangle of tubes
and someone else's child.
I whispered, "I'm sorry,"
then I leaned my head against the glass and closed my eyes.

Meditations on Death and Body Bags

KAIJA BLALOCK *Takoma Park, Maryland*

I've sometimes thought a ceremony would help, a cere-
mony surrounding a hospital death. I've even brought it up with
administration. I've worked in a hospital for a pretty long time,
long enough to remember some things being different from
what they are today. Other things haven't changed at all. We
don't have a ceremony. We do have a new logo on our sheets.
I'm very glad of one thing though; we have body bags now.
We didn't have them when I started, and I soon became very
resentful. I knew they'd had body bags in Vietnam, twenty years
earlier. Why couldn't we? Body bags are progress, no doubt
about it.

Pre–body bag postmortem procedure required at least two
people. We rolled a body back and forth on the bed between us
and slid strings and a plastic sheet underneath. The strings were
identical to those that used to hang from reels on the ceilings of
bakeries. Remember how clerks snapped them with their bare
hands and tied up a cake box? After we got the sheets and strings
under the bodies, we tied the hands together, put dentures in the
corpse's mouth if he or she wore them, wrapped the ends of the
sheet over and around and tied the strings to seal it. Wrapped
bodies usually looked sloppy. Sometimes the sheet didn't fit all
the way around. There would be discussion concerning whether
to use bows or knots or one followed by the other. Sometimes
we resorted to tape. That was in 1986.

Then came body bags, without fanfare or introduction.
Usually new hospital equipment gets hailed and praised and
announced and "inserviced" until all "affected" employees are
exhausted. They snuck body bags in. I opened a "postmortem
pack" one day and stared at the contents, confused. Something
was different. There was no plastic sheet. We had body bags
now. I ran from the utility room pulling the yellow zippered bag
out of the pack. I yelled, "Look, look!" Most people had already
seen them.

Bags. The postmortem pack also contains "toe tags" and paperwork: a death certificate worksheet, a blank death certificate, and forms allowing organ donation or autopsy. I think the forms have changed over the years, but I can't pinpoint that—the secretaries handle the paperwork.

I handle the bags themselves. I can describe them in minute detail. They're yellow. One size fits all—I've never encountered a body too long or too wide for one. They zip open and closed; the zipper is cloth. They're surprisingly heavy, and they smell like a brand new baby doll, almost like the inside of a new car. Everyone's probably smelled that smell before. Now, I involuntarily startle whenever I smell those things.

My worst moments are with bagged bodies at the elevator. Imagine waiting for an elevator, two employees making small talk and a horizontal bagged corpse under a sheet. Then, in the elevator, a violent moment—the powerful dead and the two of us and maybe someone else who came around the corner and needed to ride downstairs, all slammed up against the walls by an egotistical cadaver who lies quietly in the center, taking up all the space.

Our fear is quite simple really. Death takes away people we can't live without. And, if we didn't know them, death takes away people we wondered about, washed and talked to. Or people we didn't like and hid from. It makes them shrivel and stink.

And I know bodies stink. How? In old hospitals, the refrigeration in the morgue goes on the blink a lot. Once I encountered several of my neighbors nervously standing in front of a bush at the end of our street.

"It stinks," said one, pointing at the bush.

I sniffed. No. There wasn't a dead human being in there. I explained how I knew, and they dispersed. I've become an authority.

Odd things we end up doing for a living. Your instructors will tell you you'll get used to it, but don't believe them. Death is always shocking. My only advice to other professional death participants is: *Observe what you must, record the truth, make it public.*

In the early hours one morning, as several colleagues and I stood in a hospital room, somewhat stunned, watching an elderly woman die unexpectedly, her eyes opened and fixed on a point on the ceiling. We watched her eyes track an invisible object across the ceiling.

"There's an angel in the room," someone said. This was a moment of terrifying sweetness.

A few closing observations:

1. Most people die with their eyes closed.
2. They tend to die faster if you hold their hands.
3. I've never seen a ghost.

There are more things to say, and hopefully others will say them when they need to. Hear us out, and discuss what we say. Don't go backwards. I'm glad we have body bags now, because no one likes death. It's scary. It's sad. Admit it. Hear us.

The First Rains of April

GEOFFREY BOWE *Kent, England*

1. The Hug

    Yesterday
    For the first time
    Since I was a child
    I held my mother.

    I held her to me
    As the nurse changed
    Her bedsheet.

    I remembered how
    As a child
    She held me in her arms —
    The tears I cried then
    Extinguished
    By her warm body.

    Yesterday
    The roles were reversed.
    When I held her
    I didn't want to let go.

2. She Was in Hospital

    She was
    In hospital
    And scared
    Because this time
    She didn't think
    She would get out alive.
    Unable to move
    With no visitors

And nothing to do
But dwell on thoughts of dying.
The nurses say
That she is getting better
But they never have
The time
To stop and chat
She doesn't really
Believe them.

3.   Barely Breathing

Dying
In the afternoon
As the summer sunlight
Hits the hospital lockers.
Dying
As TV blares
In the dayroom.
People pay more attention
To an Australian "soap"
Than they do
To the person
Barely breathing
In the nearby bed.
Her life
Slipping away
As she loosens her grip
On my hand.

4.   The First Rains of April

We didn't talk
She wasn't able to anymore.
All my thoughts
Relayed to her
Through prayer and touch.
I squeezed her hand

To tell her I was there
And that I loved her.
The ventilator
Stood like a policeman
Protecting
Her injured body
While outside
The first rains of April fell
And I remembered
That it had rained
At father's funeral.

5.   In a Hospital Side Room

She was tired
And I was selfish.
She wanted to slip away
Into death
While I
Wanted to hold her here.
Her breathing
Was shallow
As I held her
For the last time
And I knew
I had to simply
Let her go.

Learning How the Bones Move

CAROL BRENDSEL *Santa Cruz, California*

Miss Mantella introduced us properly to her bones
as she displayed a skeleton on a rolling platform
that stood twelve inches above her,
had an android pelvis and a Latin name
that she mentioned as she held out the radius,
phalanges dangling,
in an improbable handshake.
Her eyes glazed as she stood beside
the empty bony cage,
as she stroked the femur and some memory ignited,
chased the shadow from that secretive sacral curve,
when flesh covered some other reckless pelvis
that hovered over her, held her,
anterior superior iliac crest to
anterior superior iliac crest.
In between the litany of names she recited —
acetabulum, trochanter, proximal, distal, innominate —
our minds wandered and imagined how she played,
Miss Mantella with her far-off stare
and floating rib of bone.

Raiment

CAROL BRENDSEL *Santa Cruz, California*

Every night I watch women try to slip out
of the body they own,
like it was a sweater or a coat
that could slink down over their shoulders and breasts,
fall off the full, child-full body
and be left draped over the edge of the bed
until all those pains and fussings
about the cervix thinning and stretching and opening
about the uterus and muscles and ligaments pulling
about the sturdy pelvis bones meant to cup and hold
a cavity replete and brimming
with organs, roped intestines, at least a five-pound purse of
    water
and the body of a child.
They want to leave all that.
Step out of those sweaty, hard-worked bodies.
Step into something cool, like a habit,
something the cloistered wear in cold stone churches.

Dear Alma Mater

RUTH E. BROOKS *Washington, D.C.*

Harlem Hospital School of Nursing, New York, N.Y., closed in 1977

Dear Alma Mater,

Rumors circulated that there were plans to close you down. They said that you had ended your period of usefulness and could no longer keep pace with the changing needs of nursing.

Through the years I had neglected you shamelessly, but I was comfortable with the knowledge that you were there. I could not envision a time when you would cease to exist. News of your impending death sank deeply into me and brought a profound sense of loss. Recently, I was informed by some former class-mates that you did indeed shut your doors. Let me tell you what part of me was sealed behind those doors.

It was in your study halls that I gave my first injection — into an orange. I remember how difficult it was to transfer that skill to a real patient; how tiny and defenseless that first patient seemed on the awesome pediatric ward.

I experienced a "coming of age" at Harlem. For me, the rites of passage involved my initiation into the world of medicine. I was lost. Now after thirty-four years of professional nursing practice, I am constantly reminded of how little I know or understand.

I have followed some of the precepts you taught and found them dependable guides for a good life and a meaningful career. I liked your concept of the importance of treating each patient as you would a guest in your own home; such a philosophy gave my nursing a kind of graciousness that few had ever seen.

I have read the Florence Nightingale Pledge, and I find its high standards not always easy to maintain. In many areas of this profession there are no easy answers for any of us. The burden of being responsible for the lives of others, often when we have little information, has weighed heavily on me. Dear Harlem, you reminded us to "loyally aid the physician in his work." You never really told us what to do if we did not agree with him.

These have not been easy years since I left the protection of your arms. I do not believe I could go through those years again, enduring the rigor of nurses' training, much less the practice of this demanding, all-consuming career. Because of the anguish and suffering of myself and others, I have been transformed.

I am indebted to you in many ways. You made it possible for me to flee poverty's relentless pursuit. I escaped from my humble beginnings, but not from myself. The fearful little myopic girl with the uncertain future is ever at my side, reminding me of the past. I keep her close to me so that I will never forget where I came from.

I shall miss you, Harlem, in a way that is too profound to put into words. A part of me was buried with you, for you have carried to your grave the rich and countless memories of my struggling years.

Hospital Flowers

CELIA BROWN *Arlington, Virginia*

Their pollen cleansed
the air of disinfectant:
the slimy green of their stink
after a few days on a ward —
Gynae, Ortho, Surgery, Med.
It really didn't matter.
There were enough to go around
when it came to flowers
around City General
as visitors left bouquets
by every patient's bed.
We never put a red and white together
(flowers of superstition,
the violence of their scent),
but mixed in a yellow or a brown:
Coral Bell, Shasta, and Mum.
Anyway, I bring the moment to you,
flowers being the only jolly job
I got to do when I was
a student nurse.
Freesia, Wallflower, Dahlia
might steal the oxygen from dreamers.
So I gathered their vases at the end of the day,
all paper bright beside a sterilizer,
their hothouse splendor not meant
for the nurse were mine.
I suds the jar again,
I wheel them out of memory,
arranging them still. As if to see
the pungent tones
that wove such a spell.

Daffodil Days

CELIA BROWN *Arlington, Virginia*

I bought the daffodils
that ward off cancer.
They are new and unopened
as a visit to the next specialist.
The flowers are shy of X-ray,
of that large pressing force
that grinds against the petals
of the body, that light reaching in,
so cold as I hold my breath.
But hope is the height of the sun
in these bare trees reeling
around me.
Will these flowers open up?
I place them in a milk glass
on the evening's edge,
do not bloom for me, I ask,
do not bloom.

Night off the Maternity Ward

CELIA BROWN *Arlington, Virginia*

There was always night's barter up on Ilkley Moor:
the glow from Keitley Arms, the smell of the mill
never quite gone from the air. The way clouds
hung down as if to fold the Old Yorkshire in its borough.
Off duty from St. Luke's, my body newly glazed,
without a thought for Maternity, I was chic in a dress
bought yesterday with my whole month's pay.
Wheel of a knee, lip-over-lip, parked for a wuthering sky,
the far city cried out to taste the night
as something there that was chance, or maybe
just the moon, glazed separately on hearts
its own pure want to be tender, tart, red, gentle, wild
or bitter as sloe-berry youth. I don't know what caused
me to stay out late, sneaking in so often
through the bars of the nurses' gate, only to look
in at the doorkeep with little or no excuse, except
for the starbloom I carried to the basket dark in my room.

The First Hour

CELIA BROWN *Arlington, Virginia*

The lie *is longitudinal,* the attitude *is one of flexion,*
the presentation *is vertex,* the position *is left occipito-anterior* . . .
   Textbook for Midwives by Margaret F. Miles

This will never happen to me
I vowed, shocked the first time
I saw a head pushing out
after a slight show & water
spurting, the attitude, right,
and the vertex coming at me —
just like it said in *Maggie Miles*

Push! I urged, sweating harder
than the woman I was trying to deliver
who wasn't listening at all
but swearing out loud
and ranting about red tomatoes
and someone stealing
out of her garden. Push!

I said it again, but by then
it didn't matter, the head
had come down and the shoulder
was presenting on its own
the little body slithered
I grabbed the greasy pole of it
upside down, clearing the airway

Cut the cord, and don't panic
I coached myself, clamping
down hard in two places to sever
the ropy tube and catch
the blue, howling vigor
of that first hour in my two hands . . .
my shaky, learning hands.

Blue Lace Socks

JEANNE BRYNER *Newton Falls, Ohio*

I am one of three nurses who work on the child
in the center of the bed. A little girl.
She is not dead yet. When we ask her to move,
only her chest rises. It is unbearable to watch.
My flashlight shows her pupils spreading
like pools of oil in her iris. Her curls are yellow.
Without thinking, I smooth her bangs across her forehead.
Her tiny body's silent. I want to put my arms around her,
tell her we are all terribly sorry for this,
and the farmer who hit her will be caught and punished,
but I don't. Then the doctor says, "She'll have to go
by helicopter." I walk her glazed mother to the desk;
she signs forms. I try to buy time with only coffee money
in my pocket. I am aware of hanging bags of clear fluid
and listening for the whisper of her blood pressure.
The copter's blades: Thump, Thump, Thump, Thump,
Thump, Thump, Thump, Thump. I believe it could wake the
    dead.
But it doesn't. The flight nurse waves through her window.
I bite my lip and pull the sheets.
Her blue lace socks hit the floor, like petals,
and their echo drowns the copter's blades.

Butterfly

JEANNE BRYNER *Newton Falls, Ohio*

The thing I keep thinking is these young men
are much too weak to make love.
These boys with yellow hair and blue tattoos
and bristly mustaches who are married
and dying with AIDS cannot enter each other
in the old way—bony hips hang,
unbeautiful, too tired to pump.

Like soft cowbells their hoop earrings
tinkle in ER, room thirteen,
as they press cool cloths to foreheads,
pass tissues for sticky green phlegm.
They wait for the doctor and lab techs
and nurses who mark their plastic name bands
with a *B*. *B* for blood hazard, *B* for boys,
B for bad. Orange-ball stickers tag
their charts; flags go up that say DANGER.

I am their nurse, and when they ask
for blankets, they cover each other the way
I spread quilts on my daughter in her crib.

They are half a butterfly on gray cement;
their skin shrinks and tarnishes,
bodies cave in, revival tents
collapsing the final week of summer.

They cough as I enter their room,
and something in me stiffens.
Even this faraway in my mask and gown
and gloves trying hard to say—*I care
that you suffer, that your cottage burns*—
its flames reach inside my tent. Whatever
chokes in this fire is large and soundless and pale.

I keep thinking as these men lift each other's
heads from the pillow, gently tilt straws
close to dusky lips, hold hands as needles
dig for veins and pull and straighten
hospital sheets hour after wounded hour—
they are migrating back to the cocoon,
the place where brown masks
protect the unbeautiful.

Red Corvette

JEANNE BRYNER *Newton Falls, Ohio*

My sister, Grace, is forty-four now, and I can't crawl into
her hospital bed to whisper secrets or slip her a half stick of Juicy
Fruit. In her blue print gown she seems a snow angel with long
chestnut hair and Mama's thin lips. When she moves, pain trav-
els like a rabid fox clawing a wire cage in her abdomen. We have
entered the forest of middle age where we will carve our initials
in the oaks, spread bread crumbs for our daughters. No more
fighting over the hairbrush or the telephone or who will dry the
dishes. No more uterus or ovaries ripe with cysts, no more pink
babies to spit up on chenille robes or split the night with three
A.M. feedings. We are past all that.

Her tray sits, a blue paper harbor full of small boats floating
gold chunks of Jell-O, grape juice, chicken broth, tea in a plastic
mug, orange ice, straws, and a single silver spoon. She tells me,
"I have no appetite."

"Please," I say, "Just a few sips of warm tea. I'll give you two
sugars."

"OK, I'll try." She exhales, too tired to fight.

After surgery, there's not much to do but hold the pan, wit-
ness dry heaves, and watch the slow strange metamorphosis of
the body healing. Over her white stockings, plastic cylinders
connected to an air compressor puff and sigh and warm her legs.
Somebody must have told her doctor that women in our family
are prone to blood clots. We buried Aunt Thelma last Novem-
ber with one that traveled from her leg to her lung. The best
Appalachian funeral I'd ever attended. As the women's choir
sang "When the Saints Go Marching In," the entire congre-
gation swayed, wanting to clap their hands in time with the
tambourine.

Without thinking, I reach for my sister's hand, and even in
this drugged meadow, her fingers respond, hang on. Dozing, the
veined azure of her eyelids becomes a curtain hiding the flicker-
ing cave of her dreams. The new scar on her belly is stapled
beneath a binder, and I'm planted in the green chair, writing my

journal. Mama's with Jesus, Father stroked, and our other siblings left this valley years ago, like it was a bite of moldy biscuit, something they needed to spit out.

It is January, and snow measures thirty inches deep on Mama's grave in Oak Forest cemetery. Where Father lives, the beaches are chilly at forty-five, and he has a cold. My sister in California complains that ninety degrees feels like the Sahara inside a glass factory. From his truck's cab, my baby brother whistles over the powdery drift he pushes. Snow in West Virginia means lots of overtime for the road crews. Deep in the coal mines, my oldest brother tries to hurry his men working the long wall; chewing the heart from a mountain takes a hard jaw.

The staff nurse enters, asks if she's finished with her tray.

"Almost," Grace answers weakly.

"Here's a pill for gas; take it after you're done." The nurse backs out of the room to her beige medicine cart.

"OK," she says, then looks at me. "They're nasty; these orange pills are really nasty."

I explain, "They're the ones that really work. Good tasting medicine is for sissies."

"Right," she nods and rolls her almond eyes toward heaven.

Her call button dangles, like a hanged man with a bloody eye, from the overhead light, six feet from her fingertips. It would take a gymnast doing a back flip to reach it. I get up, shake my head, clip it to her starched pillow case.

"How the hell do they expect you to get them with the call bell way up there?" I rant and sputter and scowl like Mama's wringer washer on winter Mondays. Grace looks at me, shrugs her shoulder.

"They're busy; it was an accident." She's absolute in forgiveness. She smiles like that August afternoon we rode home from the fair with Grandma and Grandpa Haney eating saltwater taffy by the fistfuls until we thought we'd burst.

"Will I have to go through this again ten years from now?" she asks me. "I mean, do the adhesions keep coming back?"

I'm a poet and a nurse, so she thinks I invented crystal balls. I tell her, "Ten years from now, we'll have our beach house, the wicker glider under geraniums, and a cleaning lady who comes every Tuesday. We'll shop for watercolors and pottery and rings made from agate. All the stores will be painted the colors of

Easter eggs, and we'll eat in restaurants called the *Cosmic Cafe*, *Alvin's Moon*, and *Raelynn's Pub*. We'll drink tiger milk and carrot juice by the gallons. You'll finally give up Snickers bars for celery sticks. We'll wear hot-pink bathing suits, tan as Sophia Loren in her prime. By then, I'll be teaching at Vassar or Yale, lecturing on Elizabeth Bishop, and you'll have that '65 Corvette convertible you've always wanted. When we walk the evening beach, we'll flirt with the blonde kid named Brian who wears frayed jean shorts and sells double kites from his purple booth. We'll roast hot dogs and marshmallows on the weekends when our kids come to visit. I'll play the guitar in my big gray sweatshirt, and your eyes will grow heavy while firelight dances on your face. We'll watch the sun come up like ribbons pulled from a spool while we sip cappuccino; and our hair will always be brown, brown as the walnut desk in my study, and this, all of this — the swollen bag of yellow intravenous fluid and the smell of spilled alcohol and the maintenance man with a limp buffing the floor and the knife stabbing your belly I cannot pull out — it will all be you falling off our bike, cinders in your left knee, Mama's voice above the soapy washcloth, a Band-Aid followed by a kiss."

"Whatever you say," she mumbles, squeezes my hand, drifts away, sails away, red Corvette, eighteen, soft laughter rising like bubbles blown from a plastic wand, chestnut bangs tangling in the wind.

A Story

RICHARD CALLIN *San Francisco, California*

On a gray morning
in an old woman's apartment
where he has come to wash
and pack the hole
her large right amputated toe
has left behind, the nurse sits
on a cushion's broken springs
listening as she mourns her life.

That's when he feels his skin
start to crack and peel away
from hard bone,
a summoning of grief
from the gorged chambers
where a residue has collected
of those who vanished,
forcing him as a boy
to learn that death follows love
in many forms.

And for a moment
he's wandering hills of high grass
and manzanita,
gouging his initials into root stumps
with a rusted scout blade,
listening to wasps swarm
from their hive
buried in the ground
under a plywood sheet.
He sees the valley road
twisting back from sight,
the flash of sunlight off truck hoods,
wondering how he will find his place
in the world.

The wound bed is bright red
with a white border of flesh.
He presses gauze in gently,
feeling her leg flinch in his hands,
while a story is told on a day
already half-forgotten.
Beneath a window that draws in
the city's dull glare, their bodies
sink back forever into the room.

Her leg is puffed up
and red, draining fluid
into her beige nylons,

but all she notices
is the itching, so that
every once in a while

she lifts her foot
to the stool, adjusts
the dial on the radio,

oldies, she says, *are what
makes life worth living,*
then smiles and reaches

for the spot, half-blind
with thick bifocals,
and scratches at the hole

where skin has sloughed,
says, *nothing really
keeps me down for long.*

Hospital Course

SARAH COLLINGS *Easton, Connecticut*

I remember Jagg as the epitome of the smoking issue. He was admitted to the hospital, in early December, to the cardiac floor where I work. I think it was room 644. Yes, that was it. I remember there was a fat man in the next bed. His problem was one of general excess — smoking included — but not in the way Jagg smoked.

Jagg was different. We called him Jagg because he had these sort of flapper lips and real sad-sack eyes like Mick Jagger. He was skinny like Mick Jagger too, that ropy sort of skinniness that makes me think of mad scientists or people really into yoga — people too busy to eat. When you are really skinny, your veins stick out more. When you smoke, your veins stick out more too, because your blood pressure is higher. This makes it easier to start intravenous fluids, except you have to apply more pressure to the needle as it pops through the vein wall. Smokers have tougher veins. Sometimes I can tell who's a smoker and who isn't, just by the feeling of that little pop. I'll say, "You smoke, don't you." People are always surprised that twenty years of nicotine floating around in their vascular system has had any effect at all. However, usually I know exactly who smokes and who doesn't even before I start work.

First thing in the morning, as the caffeine from my coffee hits my stomach, I pull out each chart and flip immediately to the history and physical section. I love the way the paper slides in my fingers and the way the chart always flops open the same way, right to those "risk factors." I have to see those typed words. *Positive history of smoking, two PPD.* The PPD stands for two packs per day. Sometimes it's one and a half, sometimes it's even three, or three plus. These patients intrigue me. I picture them with that ritual of the lighting of cigarettes, over and over the same way every time, like living punctuation marks, like breathing.

I remember winter nights with my brother on the back porch, that little warm glow of his cigarette in the cold, the way people will huddle around it. On that porch I had dared to enjoy watching him smoke. I think I even took a couple of drags, once.

Anyway, Jagg had flapper lips and he was skinny, and he intrigued me because he was especially young, forty-two. He had, supposedly, smoked three packs of cigarettes the night before coming in. I knew then that he was a hard-core smoker. I also knew that he would be going through withdrawal soon.

Jagg was reasonable in the beginning. He was chatty and boyish, the way he sat on the bed with his long legs crossed. He slurred his speech somewhat and had a particularly strange habit of pushing out his lower lip with his tongue at the end of each sentence and thrusting his head forward, eyes bulging a bit. He always had his belongings around him, just within reach, and he had an obsession with the type of coffee the hospital used.

"You use this?" he said that first day, the minute I walked in. "You see this? This is a disgrace." He was holding up a packet of instant coffee, the generic brand we had just switched to; the packet was a sort of sickly yellow color with brown letters. It simply said, "Coffee." He looked at me with his tongue over his lower teeth. "This coffee isn't worth anything. They switch to the cheaper kind and forget about the patient, that's what they do."

Yes, that first day with Jagg was difficult. I hated him, I guess, at first. My mother would have really . . . hated him. Common, she would have called him—the way he talked and used slang and sat cross-legged and spoke spontaneously and crudely with no introductions, no polite hellos. Yet, in a strange way, by the end of the day you couldn't help but sort of like him; he was just so strange, such a character, and so . . . unpredictable. He had a way of staring at you when you walked into the room, with a little grin, as if you were a play that was about to start. He also loved to interrupt people with ridiculous, spontaneous conclusions about life in general. I remember his saying the surgeon general didn't know anything about smoking because he had never smoked.

Jagg was definitely something else. He was fun to talk about over coffee because he was so demanding and because of the smoking thing. Everyone always asked me how he was, and if I minded having him as my patient every day, he was so weird. I like my job, but occasionally it gets routine and, well, having

Jagg around was more of a challenge; it made the day go by faster.

Toward the end of the first day, Jagg started to go through nicotine withdrawal. He first asked for a cigarette at about ten A.M. I explained the hospital policy and all the dangers of smoking—the way it constricted blood vessels, irritated the heart muscle, and all that. He seemed pretty cool about it. I gave him his Valium. The doctor had prescribed ten milligrams four times a day. He knew the guy, knew he'd be a basket case. By 11 A.M. however, Jagg started to get really agitated. He didn't understand why I just couldn't unhook him from the heart monitor and let him walk down the hall for one cigarette. One, that's all he asked for. I explained that we were responsible for him, and off the monitor we couldn't watch his heart rhythm. I guess I was intrigued, in a sick sort of way, with how he dealt with that news. He grabbed the intravenous tubing, looked at me and said, "I'll pull this goddamn thing out, you watch me." I just looked at him, and he at me. I sort of expected this.

I got an order for more Valium, which he said he'd try, but he didn't think it was going to work. Neither did I. I didn't know what was going to happen. I was intrigued still, like I said. After the first year of wacky patients and people arresting on you and bleeding and throwing up, and families screaming that primordial scream when they first discover someone is truly dead, after all that you get sort of a mechanical attitude. You feel anything could happen, and yet all you have to do is follow the policies. Everything has a policy, actually written out if you forget, in the big black policy book on the shelf in the chart room. It's a comforting feeling. So I wondered what was going to happen, but I wasn't really worried.

So, Jagg really did freak out. The next time I went into the room his heart rate was 126, and his blood pressure was 190 over 100.

"If you don't get me a cigarette, I'm going to leave. I'm going to, Christ, I'm going to kill someone." He was really yelling and pulling at his hair.

"All right," I said, "I'll call the doctor. Just hold on." I was a little nervous about his heart rate and hoped he would stay in bed long enough for me to call. It was Dr. Town that I had to call. He's funny. I hated him when I first knew him. He had a gold stethoscope that I was instantly revolted by. My mother would really have flipped about that. I mean, who did he think he was with a gold stethoscope? But after a while I began to like him, the way he flipped from his professional attitude of barking orders and demanding test results into talking about fishing. He loves fishing. Salmon fishing in the fall, those great salmon runs in New York State. He usually goes with a guide and everything, to get the best fish. I remember I once asked him about a patient, and right in the middle of giving me an explanation of aneurysms, he heard someone mention fish — it was only about the menu for the day, but that was all he needed, that one word — and he stopped, looking dazed. He then launched into a long tale about his last salmon catch. He had a picture of himself in his little fishing cap and rubber pants, standing next to the fish. You'd never believe he was a cardiologist.

So I called Dr. Town, and he was actually in a cheerful mood. He knew the guy.

"I thought this might happen," he said. "Well, look. You and I both know if this guy goes home, he's going to smoke himself to death. Let the guy have three or four cigarettes a day, will you? Just to keep him sane. I know it's against policy, but what else can we do?"

I agreed with Dr. Town. What else was there to do? So I talked it over with my supervisor. She didn't like the idea much, but I told her I didn't mind at all. I mean, if it was going to save his life. . . . We decided that everyone could pitch in and take turns walking Jagg down to the little room at the end of the hall — with a portable monitor, wheeling his intravenous nitroglycerin and praying that he didn't have chest pain or throw any clots or go into any kind of dangerous arrhythmia. I liked it, taking him down there. He would time his cigarettes out to the minute; he could just about make it on four a day.

So Jagg and I went to the end of the hall. The room was stained with ash marks and sort of dingy looking, in contrast to the other rooms that were still as new as when they were renovated. But this room was more like home, or like a bar. It wasn't the damn hospital, in that little room. I sat, after arranging the clunky IV pole and tilting the monitor so I could see it easily, across from Jagg and watched him light his one cigarette that he had saved in his hand most of the morning. He played with it nervously, stroking the paper sides. I knew it was familiar to him, the way the charts are familiar to me — like the page that told me how much he smoked — smooth against fingers, like cool shale.

Jagg lit his cigarette with a Bic lighter, with slightly shaky fingers. I love that, the beginning, the way it catches so evenly over the flat machine-made surface, the way the paper edges immediately retreat into organic, blackened curves, and the way the first tendrils of smoke sag across the room. That smell, in the beginning, is always like a campfire. Jagg inhaled with a look of relief. I thought of the smoke, going right down to every lung sac, immediately shunting into the bloodstream, then back to the heart, and wham, seven seconds to the brain.

Jagg began to talk nonstop, which was a relief because I didn't quite know what to say. It was uncomfortable, especially that first time. He knew he had caused us trouble and was breaking rules. I wasn't sure if I should look chiding, or ask him if he'd ever been to Smoke Stoppers, or what. I felt like joining in, like at a bar, when someone offers you a drink. I didn't feel like a nurse at all. Jagg was so ridiculous, he forced down boundaries, and his smoking was mesmerizing. I was tired too, sitting in that soft chair, listening to Jagg rattle on about his pickup truck and his son. I could picture them as he talked, because Jagg had a picture of his truck when it was new, and his little son with his two hands up to a loose cap, and Jagg with one hand on his son's head. I had looked for the cigarette, of course, and it was there, like a little white fish in the air, slipped between Jagg's fingers.

My mind wandered a bit, and I wasn't really listening to Jagg too well. I was thinking of the first time I had smoked. It was with Lori Field, a good friend of mine in the fifth grade. She was great — funny, talkative, always reading books and trying to be like the characters. When I knew her, she was really into Harriet the Spy books, and she even looked like Harriet a little. She was plump in a friendly way, and her feet sort of turned in. This one day, we were out in the woods behind her parents' house, and she just pulled out a pack of cigarettes like it was the most natural thing in the world to do. So Lori and I had shared one cigarette, passed it back and forth, and watched the smoke together. I thought then, sitting with Jagg, watching the monitor lights and listening to the intravenous machine, who knows, if Lori hadn't moved away, Lori and her Harriet the Spy books and her cigarettes, maybe I'd be joining Jagg right now.

So I took Jagg down to the smoking room two or three times a day, and the other nurses would take him at night. And really, if he had his cigarettes on time, he was okay. Sometimes he'd have a little chest pain afterwards, and yes, it was decided that he probably had had a small heart attack. They were keeping him on the IV until they thought they could take a look at his coronary arteries in the cardiac catheterization lab downstairs. I wondered what would happen then. He would have to lie flat for twelve hours, and he certainly wouldn't be able to smoke.

On the third day of having Jagg as a patient, I got off to a late start. It's always like that for me by the third day in a row. You get sick of work, and you find yourself answering back to patients in your head—all the things you really want to say. So I was a little tired and crabby that day. I took Jagg down for his first cigarette at ten o'clock. I remember staring at his monitor and wondering if his T waves always went up like that a little bit when he smoked. I asked Jagg if he was having any chest pain. He did his funny pout, put his hand on his chest, and shook his head. He smiled. Perhaps he thought I was too much in the nurse mode that day.

"What's the matter?" he asked. He always tried that, to smile and be inappropriately friendly, if there is such a thing. Anyway, I was a bit worried about those T waves. They didn't look right, but I decided it must be the lead placement.

At 2 P.M. we had some trouble in another room—another patient, more chest pain. I don't know. I suppose it was my fault, what happened. I was in a bad mood, a real negative mood, where I actually wanted people to come in out of the rain having chest pain and getting hooked to our monitors like laboratory animals, surprised at the proddings and pokings, and amazed at how their bodies had failed them. All the beds were full. We were short one nurse, and I was running around mechanically, sort of maniacally, one hand on my report sheet. And Jagg. He was on my mind all day; I could never forget him and when he was due for his next cigarette. He had asked me just before this trouble in the other room. I had promised to return in ten minutes.

Actually, I had been rather short with him, and he looked a bit hurt. I couldn't believe that after three days he would still get so desperate. I forgot, anyway, to go back because of this emergency, and Jagg must have been too fed up to wait. I got a call saying that Jagg was off the monitor. No big deal, really, people's leads are always coming loose. Jagg probably thought the whole monitor thing was ridiculous anyway. I logged the fact that Jagg had come loose, and eventually, say ten minutes later, went into his room. The fat man was still in the next bed. He smiled and told me that Jagg couldn't wait, he had left to smoke.

"That crazy guy took off, he couldn't wait for you," he said. I looked at the intravenous, the little pink catheter hanging from the machine, dripping precisely onto the floor at the rate of 20 cc per hour. I was so mad, I remember at first, thinking only of the time it would take to put in another IV. The least he could have done was taken the pole with him.

I started walking toward the little room. I pictured him sitting in there, grinning a little. I supposed he might have had trouble cradling that cigarette in one hand and pushing the pole with the other. I didn't blame him, really. I don't remember walking the rest of the hallway too clearly. I remember I was running, at the end, running like in a dream when you can't go fast enough, and the hall was getting longer and longer. As I walked, I heard a little sound—a kind of choke—and at the same time I had a flash of intuition about Jagg: I saw just what was going to happen to him. I started to run, afraid at first for myself and what would happen, then afraid for Jagg, for his heart, unmonitored, and what it could do unexpectedly. So I heard that little choke that people get when they're on the floor and their tongue has occluded their airway.

I could picture him perfectly even before I rounded the corner into the room, his head back, flapper lips loose, eyes dark and bottomless with fixed, dilated pupils. I felt like screaming, like the families do, I felt like running away. But there are ways to do things in a hospital, and already I was thinking of what to do next. A comfortable feeling. Phrases were going through my head, of how it would be described in the end. *An unmonitored arrest, patient noncompliant.* How long had Jagg been gone? Was it as long as ten minutes, or was it only five? If it was only four minutes, he would have a 43% chance, I remember thinking as I entered the room.

The Nurse's Pockets

CORTNEY DAVIS *Redding, Connecticut*

When patients are told they're dying
they say something simple:
I've had a good life or *Who will feed my cats?*
It seems harder on the doctor —
he waits outside the door, stalling,
until the patient confronts him.
So, Doc, they say, *What's the verdict?*

Soon, a nurse comes to bathe the patient.
There is only the sound of water
wrung from the warm washcloth,
the smell of yellow soap,
and the way she spends time praising
the valley of his clavicle, his hollow mouth.

Then, a morning when the patient leaves,
taking his body. The nurse finds nothing
but the bed with its depression,
its map of sheets she strips.
In the drawer, gumdrops. A comb
woven with light hair, and a book
with certain pages marked.

She takes all these into her pockets.
She has trunks in every room of her home,
full of such ordinary things.

What the Nurse Likes

CORTNEY DAVIS *Redding, Connecticut*

I like looking into patients' ears
and seeing what they can never see.

It's like owning them.

I like patients' honesty—
they trust me with simple things:
    They wake at night and count heartbeats.
    They search for lumps.

I am also afraid.

* * *

I like the way women look at me
and feel safe.
Then I lean across them
and they smell my perfume.

I like the way men become shy.
Even angry men bow their heads
when they are naked.

* * *

I like lifting a woman's hair
to place stethoscope to skin,
the way everyone breathes differently—

the way men make suggestive groans
when I listen to their hearts.

I like eccentric patients:
Old women who wear purple knit hats

and black eyeliner. Men
who put makeup over their age spots.

* * *

I like talking about patients
as if they aren't real, calling them
"the fracture" or "the hysterectomy."

It makes illness seem trivial.

I like saying
>   *You shouldn't smoke!*
>   *You must have this test!*

I like that patients don't always
do what I say.

* * *

I like the way we stop the blood,
pump the lungs,
turn hearts off and on with electricity.

I don't like when it's over
and I realize

I know nothing.

* * *

I like being the one to give bad news;
I am not embarrassed by grief.

I like the way patients gather their hearts,
their bones, their arms and legs
that have spun away momentarily.

At the end of the gathering they sigh
and look up.

* * *

I like how dying patients become beautiful.

Their eyes concentrate light. Their skin
becomes thin and delicate as fog.
Nothing matters anymore
but sheets, pain, a radio, the time of day.

* * *

I like watching patients die.

First they are living,
then something comes up from within
and moves from them.

They become vacant and yet
their bodies are heavy
and sink into the sheets.

I like how emptiness is seen first
in the eyes, then in the hands.

* * *

I like taking care of patients
and I like forgetting them,

going home and sitting on my porch
while they stand away from me
talking among themselves.

I like how they look back
when I turn their way.

This Happened

CORTNEY DAVIS *Redding, Connecticut*

My point is that illness is not *a metaphor . . .*
   Susan Sontag

The intern and I begin our rounds.
In room two, the intern watches me;
he doesn't like this patient anyway—

she's messy, a see-through plastic tube
pulls bile from her stomach
to a bottle near her head.

A small balloon inside her throat
keeps pressure
on vessels wrecked by years of gin.

The patient's wide awake,
but she can't talk.
I see her eyes open, her skin

pale at the moment these veins
blow, like a tire blows.
Blood backs up her nose.

She tries to sit;
her wrists are tied.
I take her hand and say, *OK. OK.*

The intern leaves.
Next the patient's gut lets go.
Stool and blood clot between her legs,

hot and soft, not like sex,
more like giving birth. *OK,* I say.
We let our fingers intertwine.

By 8:15 the woman calms.
Clots thicken in her throat;
she holds her breath.

At nine, blood coins
close her eyes. I breathe deep,
stroke the patient's arm.

The intern,
who went downstairs to sleep,
will ask me later.

But what happened here
can't be said again
and be the same.

Night Nurse

CORTNEY DAVIS *Redding, Connecticut*

Behold, the angels of God.
    Genesis 28:12

Angel,

hold their hands while I hurry
from patient to nameless patient,

feeling their skin beneath my hands
like tattered dresses stinking

of urine. Now they are sobbing.
Touch me! an old man says, *Touch me.*

The women want to steal my flesh.
They cry out, *Take my place!*

Angel, you go. Go into the corridors
where their bodies wither before me.

They die rolling in their beds,
they die sitting on their toilets.

When I try to give them breath
their vomit comes into my mouth.

Angel,

when a patient's skin is moist with pain
and pain wakes him and sings him to sleep,

when a patient's family turns away
and his hands fall empty to the sheets,

then everything is multiplied.
A sip of cold water could be a thousand lakes;

a nurse appearing uncalled in the doorway
could be someone who loves him.

Angel, when their lungs stop and their eyes
slick over and stare, when their skin

purples from toe to thumb to hollow cheek,
you be the one who gentles the world;

you be the one who stays,
all these lives flying from us.

O my body! I dare not desert the likes of you in other men
and women, nor the likes of the parts of you.
  Walt Whitman

I go on loving the flesh
after you die.
I close your eyes
bathe your bruised limbs
press down the edges of tape
sealing your dry wounds.

I walk with you to the morgue
and pillow your head
against the metal drawer. To me
this is your final resting place.
Your time with me
is the sum of your life.

* * *

I have met your husbands and wives
but I know who loved you most,
who owned the sum
of your visible parts.
The doctor and his theory
never owned you.

Nor did "medicine" or "hospital"
ever own you.
Couldn't you, didn't you
refuse tests, refuse to take your medicine?
But I am the nurse
of childhood's sounds in the night,

nurse of the washrag's sting
nurse of needle and sleep
nurse of lotion and hands on skin
nurse of sheets and nightmares
nurse of the flashlight beam at 3 A.M.

I know the privacy of vagina and rectum
I slip catheters into openings
I clean you like a mother does.

That which you allow no one,
you allow me.

* * *

Who sat with you that night?
Your doctor was asleep,

your husband was driving in.
Your wife took a few things

home to wash, poor timing,
but she had been by your side for days.

Your kids? They could be anywhere,
even out with the vending machines

working out just how much
you did or didn't do for them.

* * *

You waited
until you were alone
with me. You trusted

that I could wait and not be
frightened away.
That I would not expect

anything of you —
not bravery or anger, not even
a good fight.

At death
you become wholly mine.

* * *

Your last glance, your last
sensation of touch,
your breath

I inhale, incorporating you
into memory.
Your body

silvery and still on the bed
your lips fluttering into blue.
I pull your hand away from mine.

My other hand lingers, traces
your finger from the knucklebone
to the sheets

into which your body sinks,
my lips over yours,
my cheek near the blue

absence of your breath,
my hands closing
the silver stops of your eyelids.

The Nurse's Task

CORTNEY DAVIS *Redding, Connecticut*

When I pluck the suture
or pack the ulcer with gauze,
it becomes my task
to introduce rage to this body

that calls me, *nurse, nurse,*
as if my hands were gold.
First I cradle the body
like a mother rocks.

I lean close
and let it memorize my face.
Then, I begin.
First, something subtle.

A hasty scrape.
An accidental pinch
as if I might thrust needle
down to bone. The body

raises its hands in disbelief!
This is nothing. I thread veins
with catheters of fire,
I change morphine to milk.

When the body asks *why?*
I am silent. When the body
whines, I act bored
and turn away. If sleep comes

I sneak in and shake the body
until, angry and squinty-eyed,
it rises on its elbow
and stares at me, at last understanding

that the flesh is everything.
This is the body I love — the one
that laughs down death's trumpet.
The one that escapes.

Two Stories: 1944

EVA D. DEEB *Belleview, Florida*

Mrs. Chase and Oscar

I met Mrs. Chase a few days after I entered nursing school. She was always pleasant and cooperative, but I thought she was a little obese. She let each of us position her and bathe her, but she made no attempt to swallow the liquids or food that we offered her. She spent most of her time in bed in our demonstration room, and time after time she put up with our bungling attempts to change the bed with her in it, and she never made a sound in protest. I became very fond of Mrs. Chase, our adult female mannequin who helped us learn every new procedure. But Oscar was an entirely different matter.

I remember the day I met him. The upper class, our big sisters, had asked us for the umpteenth time, "Have you met Oscar yet?" When they thought that our curiosity had been roused to the appropriate level and the time just right, they took us to the classroom where Oscar made his home. With great aplomb, they marched to a tall green metal cabinet, opened the door, and slid Oscar out. Day and night, Oscar hung from a hook in his skull, attached to a sliding bar inside the green cabinet.

"May we present Oscar, our dear and departed! Who he is remains a mystery. Some say a handsome, smiling, nineteen-year-old male. We'll leave that up to you. May you have many happy times together."

We were taken aback, to say the least. I cringed—but soon, I was able to touch him. Oscar and his 206 bones became very familiar to me.

Out for Donuts

One quiet night, when the bright moonlight made diamonds in the crisp snow, we became very brave. We were student nurses on affiliation, doing our clinical rotation at a hospital;

studying had drained our life's juices and we needed a stimulant.

After a brief conference, we decided to send Irwin—we were known only by our last names in those days—out for donuts. Why she consented to go, I'll never know. I never would have had the nerve.

The outside doors were locked each night, but we knew how to handle that. We lived over the boiler room, a remote section of the nurses' residence of St. John's Hospital. She wouldn't be gone long anyway, we reasoned—the donut shop was only a couple of blocks away. And it was eleven o'clock. Sister Judith had already made rounds and would now be at the emergency room, where she spent the midnight hours each night. We felt fairly safe—that is until Irwin stepped out the door. It creaked loudly, like a scream in a dark deserted graveyard.

We hurried back upstairs to wait in our darkened room, where we flew to watch from the window. There she was, bundled in a big coat, a scarf wound around her head as she crunched through the snow, a solitary figure in the bright moonlight.

We sat staked out in our dark room. As we watched the bright scene outside, our stomachs began to churn. Maybe we weren't so smart after all. What if Sister Judith decided to walk our way? If she looked out the window at just the right time, she'd see Irwin coming back to the door. Then we would surely be on our way, for trouble on affiliation meant expulsion from nursing school!

After an eternity, Irwin crunched into sight again, and we raced downstairs to man the door. Again it cried out, and we froze in our tracks. But in a matter of minutes we were back in our room, consuming the greasy, indigestible donuts—the best donuts I ever ate.

The Book of God

THEODORE DEPPE *Florence, Massachusetts*

I'm thinking tonight of the three times
Marisol's tried to kill herself
before her sixth birthday—
those long suture lines on both arms—
and of the picture she cut from the *Newsweek*
I'd brought in to read on break—
I still don't know how she got it—

a photo of a crucified girl,
one of several Bosnian children
nailed to the front doors of their own homes
to frighten their parents away.
For Marisol she just hangs there
without explanation,
head bent down, black hair
falling over jutting ribs.

The single spike through her blue feet
rotates her legs inward, creating
a knock-kneed, pigeon-toed
schoolgirl of a saint.
Sacrilege, my taking down
her bedside shrine. Whole tulips
from the hospital garden
Scotch-taped around the tortured girl.

Nothing I could say about the photo's
effect on other children made sense:
she dug her nails in my wrist, tried to bite
my hand when I took the picture from her wall.
Only later and reluctantly
she accepted the spiral notepad
I gave her to write about the girl.

Her neat block letters on its cover
announced THE BOOK OF
GOD CAME BACK AS A SMALL GIRL.
She didn't want words inside, only pictures.
Tonight I can't stop imagining
photos crowding that bright red notepad.
Working with her scissors and tape,
Marisol sits on a bed in her foster home,
feet tucked under her, completing her book.

Admission, Children's Unit

THEODORE DEPPE *Florence, Massachusetts*

Later, I'd look up the story a friend told me years ago,
how St. Lawrence taught his disciples to recognize the smell
of sin, how they'd set off in pairs through the Roman Empire,
separating good from evil, hoping to speed the Lord's return.
It must have been this scrap of legend, half-remembered,
that moved in me last week when I stopped suddenly and,

trying not to stare at the woman, drew my breath in and smelled
her, catching a scent that was there and then not there.
She was telling me how her son set fire to his own room,
how she'd found him fanning the flames with a pile of comics,
and what could she do with such a child? Her hair
was pulled back in a ponytail, her face shining and suffering,

and what she had done, it turns out, was hold her son down
so her boyfriend could burn him with cigarettes.
The details didn't, of course, come out at first, but I sensed
    them.
The boy's refusal to take off his shirt. His letting me, finally, lift
it to his shoulders, examine the six wounds arranged in a cross,
raised, ashy, second or third degree, I don't know which.

Silence in the room, and then the mother blaming
the boyfriend, blaming the boy himself.
I kept talking to her in a calming voice, straining for something
I thought I smelled beneath her cheap perfume — a scent
maddening, of course, because nameless, little top note
of thrill followed by something — how can I describe this?

a bass note after, or under, the other smells, as if something
not physical had begun to rot.
I'd like to say all this happened when I first started
to work as a nurse, before I'd learned not to judge the parents,

but this was last week, the mother was crying,
I thought of handing her a box of tissues, and didn't.

When the Romans crucified Lawrence, according to the story
even the church won't stand behind anymore, he asked Jesus
to forgive him for judging others when his own sin was so large.
He wept on the cross because he smelled his own soul
and knew he was lost. Only when the soldiers lifted him down
did they find rose petals, clutched in his fists,

a new species exuding a fragrance never before smelled on earth.
The boy got up, sullen, wordless, brought his mother
Kleenex from my desk, pressed his head into her side.
Bunched the bottom of her sweatshirt in both hands
as if anchoring himself to her. Glared at me.
It took four of us to pry the boy from his mother's arms.

Thallium Scan

THEODORE DEPPE *Florence, Massachusetts*

(for V. T.)

The vivid shades of the scintillation camera
are not the colors of our world: the heart's
failing pump reflected in molten tones
that spell a passing, a brilliant orange fist
opening and closing, over and over,
like a screen door slamming itself shut
in an empty farmhouse. So that we think each time
the door swings open we should be able to see out —

and yet the scanner shows only the heart.
It is all mapped out, in thallium,
without the mansions, without the many
rooms or windy fields. It misses
the canopy of fire raised all around us,
illuminating the darkness, where we live.

Gloria

THEODORE DEPPE *Florence, Massachusetts*

The photograph in this morning's *Chronicle*
shows the steeple of Willimantic's Congregational Church
toppling in the '38 Hurricane, a shot that means

someone stood on Valley Street during the storm's height,
captured the exact moment the spire buckled
over its tower, poised above an elm also gone now.

Imagine that unidentified photographer, shielding the lens
with his hand, waiting on the deserted street for—what?
the steeple's fall? or the power hidden in this world

to manifest itself, an act of God we say
because like God we think we cannot know ourselves
without it. Three years ago

patients slept in beds we'd pulled to the hall
the night Gloria approached. As wind battered glass,
I played gin with a pianist from East Hartford—

we might have been old friends, sitting up late
in some all-night cafe, though I was the one
that day who found his hidden syringe.

Watching from the wire-and-glass window, we worried
for our families, but when I pointed out the snowplows
brought to clear September roads of pine boughs and debris—

those blue sparks the steel plow struck from blacktop—
he sensed my love of storms, turned to me, half-smiling,
asked how much damage it would take to really satisfy me.

Gooseberries

THEODORE DEPPE *Florence, Massachusetts*

For the first time in weeks, staying up all night on suicide watch,
I find I'm happy. My job is to pay attention,
which I can do listening to Coltrane on the radio, quietly

so as not to wake Luke, the nine year old just an arm's length
     away.
I scan his homemade quilt for movement, recalling the girl who
     years ago
sliced her wrist with a thumbtack while the nurse by her bedside

watched but couldn't see. I'm grateful for a few hours to read,
a story by Chekhov in which Ivan Ivanovitch's brother achieved
his life's goal — tasting gooseberries grown on his own land.

But the story is really about Ivan, how he sees that his brother's
     happiness
ignores the grief of those around him. *How many satisfied, happy
     people
there really are!* he thinks. *What a suffocating force it is!*

Luke wakes from a nightmare of his father
that for a minute doesn't stop even after he sits up,
but he's exhausted, falls back to sleep, and I return to my chair,

the open volume of Chekhov like a small tent before the dark
     corridor.
When Luke was three, his father hit him with a baseball bat,
left him comatose for a month.

On his sixth birthday, Luke slashed his forearm, prayed for a
     long time
that he would die. Angels with red wings
corner him now when he is alone. Last evening in the shower

they made him pummel his face until the aide found him.
I don't want a life that's walled off from such pain,
and yet I don't want my old cult of suffering, either.

Tonight I envy what Chekhov, who once traveled 6,000 miles to
    Siberia
to talk with each prisoner on Sakhalin Island, tasted
years later, the night before his body was carted back to Moscow

in a dirt-green van marked *Oysters*. Knowing he would die
before his doctor's oxygen arrived, he sent downstairs for
    champagne —
Such a long time since I've tasted champagne!

The Gift: La Cumbre, Guatemala

ELIZABETH DESIMONE *Seattle, Washington*

As the end of our day in La Cumbre, Guatemala, neared, I was exhausted. One more mother carrying a baby wrapped in a shabby blanket caught my attention—except this mother clutched her baby and paced. She said nothing, but her expression said, "I know we didn't get here in time for clinic, but my baby . . . *por favor, Señorita.*" How could we refuse? I sighed, knowing I'd have to take the time to screen her, to see what the baby had. Thank God, this was the last patient to see.

Fay, my coworker, Tox, our translator, and I regularly visited La Cumbre for clinic and health classes. Ladinos and the K'ekchi Indians populated the small town. They didn't quite trust us yet, two foreign missionary nurses. Some utilized our clinic and attended classes, but the majority stayed away. They believed the pastor of the Evangelical Church who said we gave out dangerous medicine; he accused us of being mixed up with the devil. Sometimes we heard him shouting these remarks through a megaphone to the people in town at the bottom of the hill.

Even the Catholics were leery and made us set up our clinic in a three-sided shelter, poor cover from the hard winds and sudden bursts of rain. At night, however, they let us sleep inside the church. Like the shelter, it was built of vertical branches with a dirt floor, covered by a thatched roof. On hot days after morning clinic, we took naps on homemade benches in the cool, quiet church. For clinic, we moved the benches outside to the shelter, using some to line up the bottles of antibiotics, cough syrup, iron and vitamin pills, and others for people to sit on as they waited their turn.

La Cumbre consisted of a few *tiendas*, small stores stocked with meager supplies of Coca-Cola, plastic bags of sugar, soap powder, and rubber sandals. A scattering of thatched-roof houses seemed to be plopped at random in the hills. The church perched on the highest hill overlooking the sleepy little town.

Sometimes at dusk I sat outside the church on fallen logs and watched the gorgeous red sunset. Carrying our equipment up the steep hill made me sweat and complain—but it was prettier up there, surrounded by the dense greenery of the jungle.

I quickly finished with the child I was examining and rose to question this mother whose worried face made me uneasy. I unwrapped the blanket. Inside, a baby boy gasped for breath; his face was dusky blue. Mucus gurgled with each labored breath.

For a second I couldn't move. Then I snatched him from his mother's arms and rushed to our makeshift table. *Por qué no me dijo que era tan enfermo . . .* "Why didn't you tell me he was so sick?" I yelled over my shoulder.

With one hand I swept instruments aside and laid him down. I lifted his chin to extend his neck—when I opened his mouth, I saw his throat drowning in thick yellow mucus. I reached in with my fingers and tried to pull out the ropes of stringy phlegm, but it was so thick it couldn't be moved.

"Fay. Hurry. Get the bulb syringe! Tox. The emergency box!"

Tox froze momentarily. Then he jumped into action, assembling the IV equipment. He hammered a nail into the shelter wall to hang the IV bottle, while I hollered instructions.

Fay bent over the little form. She tried to suction his mouth with the bulb syringe, but no mucus came through—it was too thick. We used bulb syringes in the States to clear the noses of newborn babies—they weren't meant to cope with this horribly obstructed airway.

"God, oh God." Fay's words ended in a sob.

The baby's feather heart beat so fast I couldn't count. His breathing sounded like someone gargling. Fay placed her lips over his nose and mouth and blew. Over and over, she tried. She straightened up. "Nothing. I can't get any breath through." My despair was reflected in her face.

"Keep breathing. We have to keep trying!" I could hardly get the words out.

Tox stood by helplessly, his normally stoic expression pinched in concern. I looked up once. The shelter was crowded with people too curious to leave.

I couldn't stop trying. Before Guatemala, I had worked in an emergency department for years. There, everything conceivable was done to save a life. If only we had better equipment! This never would have happened in the States. We continued to work over the baby.

After what seemed like an hour but was only a few minutes, his chest stopped moving, and he lay lifeless before us. Fay and I, and many of the men, women, and children stood together with tears running down our faces. I smoothed back the soft dark hair from his forehead, then wrapped the blanket around him. Such a beautiful baby. I hugged his mother as she sobbed in my arms.

Lo llevo al doctor en San Luis . . . "I took him to the doctor in San Luis. I gave him cough syrup four times a day, just like he told me, but it didn't help. The doctor said come back if he wasn't better, but the trip costs so much. Every day he got sicker." She buried her face in the baby's blanket.

That day, she went on, he had gotten worse. She brought him to us, thinking we might help.

"I didn't think he was going to die. He was so healthy looking, wasn't he, Señorita?" It was true. His clothes were patched, but clean. He was chubby, as an eight month old should be, with velvety chestnut skin.

I thought of so many things as she told her story. Why wasn't an antibiotic prescribed? The likelihood of complications was great in this disease-prone population. Why had the mother stood by while Fay and I examined patients who had nothing more than worms? Couldn't she have come earlier? I blamed myself too. Why didn't I look up sooner? With a few extra minutes, could we have saved him?

Slowly, people drifted away. Neighbors led the mother home, as Fay and I began to clean up the mess. Someone said there'd be a prayer service later that night in the baby's home.

"Maybe we should cancel our classes," I suggested to Don Julian, the catechist. "It doesn't seem right to teach a class on nutrition now." But Don Julian told us to go on as planned.

We fixed a simple dinner. No one said much while we waited for class to start, each of us locked in our private sadness. I kept seeing the baby's face, and I felt like crying again. The disgust I was beginning to feel for those running this government, the ones who could do something to provide better healthcare, grew even stronger. I thought perhaps a few people might come to class, but that most people would be with the baby's family.

As 7 P.M. approached, people began arriving. Soon the shelter was full of men, women, and children, both Ladino and K'ekchi, and a crowd stood at the back. We never had such a turnout in

La Cumbre. Fay and Tox and I looked at each other, amazed. The people of La Cumbre were giving us the gift of their presence. I felt as if comforting arms were embracing me; my depression lifted.

While Fay and I expounded on the merits of breast milk and Tox translated, I looked out at the people listening with total attention and courtesy, their expressions the most humble I had ever seen. My fatigue melted away.

After class, we walked down the hill single file along a dark path lit only by our bobbing flashlights. Tox seemed to know the way. We arrived at the house where everyone gathered.

Inside, we were welcomed as if we were royalty. A man rose and motioned me to sit on his stool, and a woman insisted that Fay take the only other stool in the house. The baby, dressed now in finer clothes, lay on a rough wooden table in the center of the room. The table was covered with a white cloth, and white flowers wound in a crown through his dark curls. White candles burned on each corner of the table, and shadows flickered on the stick walls and straw roof. On a bed next to the baby lay his brother and sister, asleep.

Don Julian stood. *Hermanos en Cristo, vamos a rezar.* He made a sign of the cross, then sank to his knees and began to pray. *Padre nuestro* . . . "Our Father. . . ." People around me knelt and I followed them. The grainy dirt bit into my knees. Instead of praying, I thought about how these people accepted whatever life brought to them. In that simple house, peace surrounded me.

Afterward, we wound our way back up to the church, a black silhouette at the top of the hill. "I wonder where the mother got money for that cloth and the new clothes?" I asked Tox.

"The neighbors. Someone else paid for the candles. *Así se hace.* That's how it's done."

That day marked the beginning of change in La Cumbre. We no longer heard a word about bad medicine. From then on, we had so many patients we couldn't see them all.

Mr. Death

R. ERIC DOERFLER *Harrisburg, Pennsylvania*

Mr. Death came to sit with me.
I was in a cafe
having a coffee and
there was music.

He said,
"It was black as oil, wasn't it.
The cancer. Thin and dark like, say,
balsamic vinegar."

I jerked my head toward him and
he sat down.
There were empty tables nearby
but he sat with me.

"Horrible smell, cancer,"
he added.

Who are you? Get away from my table!

"*Your* table? I don't see your name on it.
In any event, remember, you'll be dead one day,
and then it won't be *your* table anymore."

I was going to hit him, but I couldn't. Something he said.
I let him sit.

He said:
"God, how I hate being the enemy." For
my benefit, I think — although
he stared ahead into the passers-by as he said it.
"You cannot know —"

If this is that same tired bullshit about
how lonely it is to be Death, spare me. I've heard it.

"Ahh, yes of course. Movies?"

I don't know . . . movies . . . books.

"You're right. What's the difference . . . ? So, you're in
the business? Mortician?

A nurse . . . what's the difference to you?

I sipped my coffee. The warmth of it slipping into my mouth
reassured me, as did the slight springtime nip. My eyes
followed the naked legs of a young woman.

Death's eyes were on mine. I was uncloaked.

"Yes. She has it."

Cancer?

"What else? She will learn of it tomorrow. Today is her
last day of freedom. Actually, the biopsy won't be in for
a week. A pap test. What a boon . . . medical tests."

I understood — and said so: *It's not the lives, it's the*
suffering. Isn't it?

The gentleman signaled the waitress and ordered an espresso.
I found that funny. *In a hurry?*

"Our work. It's not easy work, is it?"

He knew the soft places.

"The stench, the crying and wailing . . . you know, I'm exhausted
at the end of a day. This is hardly a life."

We sat in silence for some time. Mr. Death sipped his espresso. His thin lips so gently on the rim of the cup, the steam in his nostrils, rich and bitter. So many people passed us I could not count them. I wanted to. Some dark tally. But after moments, I lost track. The coffee was delicious, the air perfect, mad with the noise of life. I lost track.

He finished, and it had only seemed like a moment.
Going?

"Must."

I watched him fade into the crowd. Not so much as good-bye, happy hunting . . . whatever. As if he hadn't sat down at all.

My gaze fell to the cup with its dregs, black and oily in a crescent at the bottom. I thought of the woman and how it waited within her silent body, corpulent with the wet black tumor. The way we would wrap her in white plastic before committing her to the hearse.

I was glad he stopped by.

First Night Duty — 1950

JANE FARRELL *Green Bay, Wisconsin*

"Here!" Cele pokes the cold flashlight
into my colder palm,
shoves me out into the hallway first
because I am smaller.
Two rustling student ghosts
with caps, legs, and feet,
we creep through the darkness
of old St. Mary's second floor
to check our patients.
Ours. We shiver.
I flick the switch of the flashlight
off and on as we follow
the short, faltering beam in and out
of rooms made darker
by the small circle of yellow
under the night lamps.
I shine the light on smooth
or crumbled mounds of bedding.
We stand still until
our own breathing catches
the rhythm of the body underneath.
Relieved, we move on.
In the doorway of 203,
my thumb *click click* on the flashlight.
Blackness.
The radiator clanks and hisses
at our frozen ankles,
we move and bump each other.
I peer ahead,
see a massive tombstone on the bed!
A hand clutches my throat,
squeezes a scream into a gasp.
Cele trips, trapped by a shadowy form.

In my shaking hand, the flashlight
begins to flicker,
throws a feeble ray onto the bed.
The tombstone collapses.
Fingers on my throat fall away.
In my head, I hear an echo:
graveyard shift.
GRAVEYARD SHIFT. I say it out loud,
but not as loud as the thump
and swish of Cele, untangling herself
from a bedside curtain,
and only a whisper, caught
in the rise and fall of a midnight snore.

In Common Darkness

HELEN TRUBEK GLENN *Litchfield, Connecticut*

In the school for deaf-blind children
everything is by touch. *Susan uses her lower lip
as a sense organ*, kissing the world
without judgment. Her face close to the edge
of the classroom table, she breathes and pushes
against the tangy film of cold moisture.

Tommy wears a carapace,
like that of the sea tortoise
struggling back to the beach,
to stop him from banging,
banging his head for the *stims*.
At night he curls up under the pressure
of all that lack of sound, like a small
question mark in common darkness.

The golden child, flaxen-haired Cecily,
a pleasure to watch, the teachers
thinking, "If only," dressed brightly
by her mother in pinks and yellows
like jiggly butterscotch pudding,
the one thing she's learned to sign,
I'd rather be eating pudding!
Her fingers practiced in these words,
perhaps she feels the vibrations
of laughter at her only joke.

But today she swims again to the far end
of the pool, sinks into ten feet of water.
Through the ripples her face is the image
of a visionary fourteenth-century

saint seeing Paradise. Her teacher, rising
to save her, knows the child remembers
deep water pressing on her skin *creates
a marvelously pleasant sensation.*

justanurse

CHRISTINE GRANT *Wynnewood, Pennsylvania*

when i was 5 my mother ("I'm-turning-30")
decided i was to be a nurse, "comfort-cleanliness-in-white."
so for Christmas i posed by the tree,
starched cap, blue-red-lined cape, cradling
   "HeddagetBeddadoll."

when i was 15 my books were "nurseslovingnursing,"
weekends were "pink-white-candy-striped" volunteering.
so for Christmas i posed by the tree
at the nursing home, next to wheelbound-hopelessly-exhausted.

when i was completed and assured, initialized and indexed,
i knew i was of inestimable value, trained-registered-certified.
so for Christmas i posed by the tree,
with my daughter, a stretched-stained-infunky-wrapped-5
   (on 25).
      "Can't even be a nurse," initiated straightness,
         "they never dance in the halls."

when I was "40plusnotsobad," i stepped back to watch nurses
ministering care and comfort, a gentle untitled dance.
so for Christmas i posed by the tree,
. . . "justanurse" . . .

The Gift

CHRISTINE GRANT *Wynnewood, Pennsylvania*

A dull, crude bellring invaded my slumber. Such a struggle to get out of bed. I wanted not to wake but to burrow deeper down into the covers where no alarm would ever reach me. Why had I agreed to do a double shift? This damp, chilly October Saturday was meant for hot coffee and bagels, perhaps a half hour of some ridiculous cartoon with my six year old. I struggled through the ritual of dressing for work, with the fleeting thought that I was almost thankful for the ease of a uniform. I tried to create an illusion, to trick myself into believing it was another normal day. But the house was so quiet, and the car started slowly; was it a sign?

Driving to work was a chore. The miracle of a "transit trance" didn't work—no one else was on the road. I was out of sync with the lights, and the blocks seemed longer than necessary. From a distance the hospital looked plain, almost stark. My coffee, in a plastic container with an opening so small I couldn't taste the brew, was getting cold. Inside, the corridor lights hummed a mournful tune, and the bulletin board messages were old, left over from the dog-eared days of August. I turned the radio on for company and started reading the notes from the night before. My fingers were drumming an erratic rhythm on the counter that cheered me up a little when the phone rang.

"Anne." My husband's voice. "Anne, there is horrible news."

I was annoyed. I wanted to hear this news quickly, solve whatever problem he had, and get back to work. I took a short sip of coffee and grimaced. I had forgotten how cold it was.

"Elizabeth is dead. Oh my God, Elizabeth is dead," he stuttered into the phone.

Who is this prank caller, I thought. Who would dare tell me such small-town news when I got up early on a Saturday morning to be at work? Who was giving me such a bad memory?

"Did you hear me? Anne? Your brother found Elizabeth this morning in her crib. They found her dead."

I wanted to scream. I wanted to scream and scream. I laughed at myself. I didn't know how to scream—I'd never had to. I had never had a "scream" situation. I hung up the phone and scanned my memory in a frantic attempt to recall when I last saw Elizabeth, what I had learned from her, what I had consumed from her life that would give me the words to say to my brother, her father.

I will never remember what I said to my brother that gray morning. But I know I no longer like Halloween. I no longer like autumn. I no longer like the hospital on Saturdays. I know I hate my coffee cold.

The phone calls were an endless winter. My family thinks they are "good" in a crisis. We have invested heavily in ourselves as good stock, thinking that our exteriors match our inner workings. We pride ourselves on being people of few words, with little emotion, and less need for each other. Nevertheless, we are a big family, the kind that needs a lot of chairs around the table, plus a card table for the little ones. I pictured all of us together; together we could make her death less. I was wrong.

As a nurse, my experience with death has always been so professional, so controlled. I graduated believing that death was a curiosity that no-family-of-mine would suffer. Now, for Elizabeth, I wanted to be clinical. I wanted to give "therapeutic" handouts. I didn't *want* to be comforted.

But the group of people gathered at my brother's home was so good at comforting. They looked beyond the tears that made the skin on my face look old. They ignored the blue lines in my eyelids. I suffocated as whoever-they-were looked into my eyes and chanted the painful truths: "I am *so* sorry." "I know you will miss her so much." "A little girl shouldn't die." I couldn't breathe. I turned cold as their words resounded hypnotically in my brain. I swayed in the tenor of their voices.

The day of the funeral Elizabeth lay in her casket and I stroked her arm. *How unusual that a baby could be so good.* She had quiet toys and baby-stained blankets around her: Raggedy Ann and Andy smiled, and a rather plain rabbit lady made by Grandma guarded Elizabeth's thighs. Leaves, rocks, earthly possessions, and my surreal thoughts took up the unused portions of the little white box. Of course I knew about children dying in their sleep. I had heard stories of such pain, I had attended those who died and those who grieved; now I knew I was an amateur.

I scrutinized my brother from across the room. His grief seemed to come in waves, like the angry waters of childhood that slap against sunburned knees. *Ride this one out. Ride this one to shore.* I gulped back my anger. I was mad that I grew up in Iowa, that I didn't know more about the ocean. Why couldn't I stir memories of sitting, warm on the wet sand? I left the drone of mourners, wondering who could close the casket on a little girl.

The funeral was deviltry. I wanted to run wild, to leave and browse at an outlet in the mall, to offer an impromptu party. My brother passed out bubblegum. Did I hear him say that Elizabeth had just learned not to swallow the sweet elastic? I took the piece thrust in front of me. Chew, chew. Chew it hard, I thought, bite your tongue. Bleed. Show them the raw wound and extract the pain. *Let it be me you prepare to bury!* No one was listening.

After the ceremony, we returned to Elizabeth's house. Her bedroom door was shut. I wanted to crawl into her crib, still unmade from that morning. If I went into that room, I thought, everyone will watch me, so I searched the room for diversion and saw my new brother-in-law. He was maliciously humorous, unknowingly attacking our family with his stories and his I-haven't-laughed-this-hard-since-high-school craziness. He had no idea yet that we couldn't do death with any style. For a moment he made me forget what I dreaded—the thought of comforting my brother.

I fled the house, longing to be safely alone in my car, but my brother stood in the driveway. I shook off thoughts of Elizabeth, the image of her in the ground, the decay of her short life, the rain soaking deep into that white tomb.

I placed my arms awkwardly around my brother and stiffened, ready for whatever words he could loan me, but instead I felt myself being rocked as he held me tightly.

Don't let me go. His breath on my neck was even, warm, and I closed my eyes. At last we could have our pain; we no longer needed to instruct ourselves how.

"I love you," he whispered for both of us. His voice echoed down my spine.

We pulled apart. No smile, no glance cheapened by acknowledgment. Just clear silence. A gift from Elizabeth.

Dehiscence

AMY HADDAD *Omaha, Nebraska*

You have come unstitched.

Holes appear on your threadbare abdomen.
Tunnels develop and connect bowel, liver, pancreas.
Enzymes ooze out and digest your skin,
no matter how hard we try to stem the flow.
Mounds of dressings,
miles of tape — a jury-rigged system to
hold together our mistakes.
The stench is overwhelming, ever present,
reminding everyone, but especially you,
that you have come undone.

Since I cannot bear your suffering,
since the truth is too horrible to grasp,
since I can offer you nothing else,
I clean you up.
I wash your face,
brush your teeth,
comb your hair,
turn you gently on your side,
push soiled linens away,
roll clean sheets under you,
remove layers and layers of damp, disgusting dressings,
and replace them with new dressings and tape.

Since I am helpless in the face of your tragedy,
I give you the certainty and calmness of my motions,
the competence and comfort of my touch
as I smooth the top sheet over my work.
Done.
For a few pristine moments, we allow ourselves
to be caught in the illusion of your wholeness.

Thoughts on V-Tach

MITZI HIGLEY *Memphis, Tennessee*

O favorite heart!
Irritable heart
Silently beat, steady on
or flutter faint and sweet
Frighten not—a skip or two
race me away
on a silver bullet
I'll never see

Take me
with earrings, lip gloss
and silver tresses
unaware in my boots-on day
clean
and clear away

Dead Dog Days

(A man with AIDS talks of his dog)

NINA HOWES *New York, New York*

He was an amazing dog, very strong, like me. I'm built like an ox. Nothing can get me. It's that sturdy Polish stock. We come from a long line of peasants. You should see my mother — talk about a big woman. I always told her she would outlive me. Well, we'll see. My dog, Waldo — he was something. If I had the time, I would have trained him. He could've been on the David Letterman show. He was so strong he could open the refrigerator door. The meat, the chicken — he would just take it out of the refrigerator and eat it. I had to get a padlock and put it on the door. There was no other way to stop him. At night, if I was watching TV, he would sit by my feet and stare at the TV like he was part of the family. I think he thought he was a person. He never liked being around other dogs — he'd snap at them. But people — he'd run right up and sniff them and lick them — he was all over them.

When he died I was heartbroken. I felt like I had really lost a friend. He died in my arms. He had been sick and his breathing was getting shorter and shorter, like gasps. I was holding him when he took his last breath. I didn't know what to do. I wrapped him in a towel and laid him in the back of the car. I bought several flowered plants and drove to the family plot in Queens. I got out and started digging with my spade. People passing by thought I was simply arranging the plants. But I dug deep enough to lay Waldo there. Then I covered him and fixed the plants around him. I wanted him near me, so we can be together when I die. Well, maybe. I'm a fighter, nothing's going to stop me.

Ricky T and His Cockatoo

NINA HOWES *New York, New York*

"Bye, Bye," she hawked. "Bye, Bye!" Ricky T introduced
me. "That's Vanessa, she's very jealous of other females. One
time she flew on this lady's head and tried to attack her. That
was funny." I didn't think it was so funny. I moved my chair
away from her perch. "Don't worry," he said, "her wings are
clipped. She can't fly far now." "What do you want! What do
you want!" she squawked. Vanessa had hopped from her perch
and was now clawing her way down the side of a gray wicker
chair, closer to me. I moved again. "What do you want! What do
you want!" "Your temperature," I said. She cocked her head
intently as if she really had to think about this. "She likes to sing
Ave Maria," Ricky told me. "Come on Vanessa, sing Ave Maria."
She sang two notes and then decided to stop. "You see, that's
how she is," Ricky explained. "When you want her to do some-
thing, she won't do it. But if you're on the phone, she'll sing
loud as day." I began to sing Ave Maria. Vanessa tilted her head.
"Well, she didn't gong you," Ricky said. "If she doesn't like what
you're doing she'll go eeeck!" "Bye! Bye!" she said. "Okay, I'm
leaving now." Ricky escorted me down the hall to the door. "She
gets nervous when I leave the room with another woman." And
soon enough I heard her yell, "Get back here! Get back here!"

Miranda's Dream

NINA HOWES *New York, New York*

I have this dream — like a nightmare it comes to me. My husband's brother — oh, he was gorgeous, big shoulders, tall, sturdy — before he got sick. He's dead now. And in the dream I know he's dead. And I'm waiting for the bus. I have to go somewhere. He appears — and I say, "What are you doing here? Aren't you dead?" He just smiles at me and tells me he is doing well, and he is going to give his wife a baby. His wife never had a baby. She's a dancer and she was always having miscarriages or something. And I get so nervous because I know I have to get the bus, but here he is. When he was alive he used to come over almost every day. I would cook breakfast for him and my husband — bacon and eggs. And then they would go out together. My husband loved him. They were good friends. Sometimes I would go out with them. My husband on one side and my brother-in-law on the other. My husband's skinny but he looks good. Here I was surrounded by two gorgeous men. I felt so hot. He's the one who used to tell us don't drink, don't smoke. And now he's the one who's dead. Where is his picture? I have to show you.

I Drive in the Lane

GEORGIANA JOHNSON *Port Matilda, Pennsylvania*

I drive in the lane.
A new calf glistens in the sun, tries to stand and stumbles,
umbilical cord still swinging.

I approach the gray weathered house and the smell assaults my
    nose before I reach the door.
Human feces and rotting food.
A naked woman sits, barricaded in a darkened room bare of any
    furniture other than a bed with a plastic tarp covering the
    mattress.
Her husband sits in a chair, his left side useless, the residual
    effects of a stroke.
"I can't handle her anymore," he says. "She runs away."
She smiles as I enter, an empty smile,
a void behind those watery blue eyes that look into mine.
She stands and hands me her clothes in a bundle like a gift.

Has she been fed?
Does she get her medicine?
Who helps clean her?
"Have you tried Swiss Miss Hot Chocolate?" he responds.

I clean her: a difference comparable to moving one grain of sand
    from one section of the beach to another.
The Office of Aging says it's not a crisis.

As I drive back up the lane, the calf is on its feet.

Cats

GEORGIANA JOHNSON *Port Matilda, Pennsylvania*

Old people and cats seem to go together well.

There were big old cats who lay curled under a wood stove and maintained aloof control over their surroundings.

There were younger working cats who were expected to catch rodents for their keep.

There were the frisky kittens who would tear at my stockings and bat at my stethoscope.

There were the cats who would hide under a table or chair and those who would follow my every move and be quite verbal about my intrusion into their domain.

There was the smell of cats.

Old women would talk about their cats as if they were children.

Old men would pretend not to like the cat while they lovingly stroked its back with their chapped hands.

I would frequently have to say hello to the cat before my visit was considered complete.

I have a theory that old people and cats go together so well because people live longer if there is a cat in the house.

I doubt I can prove this, but I keep two on hand, just in case.

Christmas Time

GEORGIANA JOHNSON *Port Matilda, Pennsylvania*

Always!
I mean every house.
A package under the tree for the visiting nurse.
Cookies, candy, Avon perfume, cookies, a scarf, a hat, cookies,
  gloves, mittens, cookies, nut bread, cookies,
once a bottle of homemade wine from a great old Italian man,
  cookies, ornaments made from beads and old egg cartons, a
  pen, cookies, a book of ideals, cookies, home-canned goods,
  eggnog, crocheted slippers, cookies, homemade bread and
    lots of hugs.
    And did I mention cookies?

About Nursing

MICHAEL KELLY *San Leandro, California*

It's the secrets people tell me
that I like the best.
  All the dirty laundry that needs airing
about the substances and people
they abused.
  Love turned to hate: control dominance
ruthless business ventures
        pouring their hearts
        spilling their guts
about how they
  cheated at what, on whom,
    and why.
  The things they wanted, lusted after
got and lost . . . the people, the relatives
  friends fucked over just to get
  something, somewhere, somebody
tainted and tawdry, every day
is Yom Kippur . . . every evening
Good Friday Confessional
  the nights are even more insane
  irrational and unbelievable.
The Bad thing is I can't really
  tell you mine
By the way what's yours
I'm not in it for the money
I'm in it for the secrets

While His Life Went on Around Him

ANGELA KENNEDY *Essex, Great Britain*

I seemed to run into Darren every time I got out of my car in the hospital car park. He would swagger over from nowhere with an entourage of mates and accompany me into work, pestering me for a date. He asked me three times before I took him up on his offer. "Pick me up at eight," he said, and I remember thinking, oh no, not another fella without a car.

As it turned out, Darren had been banned for drinking and driving. He had been in prison as well. I went back to his place for coffee, and he gave me his current defense draft to read. This time he was being done for breaking and entering a builder's yard.

But in spite of this, I liked him, so for three whole weeks I saw quite a bit of him. I even met his mother. But Doreen didn't seem too impressed with me. When we were introduced, she nodded but hardly looked at me, just snapped at Darren for taping over her video recording of *The Thorn Birds*. She actually worked at the hospital as a domestic in the geriatric unit. But I had never seen her there. A few minutes after we met, she threw on this awful sheepskin coat, bunched up her bleached hair, dark at the roots, into a rubber band, and went off, to bingo, I supposed.

Yes, for three whole weeks Darren and I became quite close. But then, suddenly, Darren cooled off, about the same time I said that I wasn't ready to sleep with him just yet. But I could not afford to get upset at romantic setbacks. I had a new job in the intensive care unit at the hospital. I was now a staff nurse. A real feather in my cap that was, reward for my three years away from home in Wexford, slogging my guts out in the wards and the School of Nursing library in a grimy London hospital.

It may have been a feather in my cap, but it was a terrible place to work in, that intensive care unit. Everyone seemed to have it in for me. Insolent enrolled nurses constantly questioning what little authority I had, making it impossible for me to get my job done properly. Pushy, snooty physiotherapists with degrees in arrogance and with tans stolen from the ultraviolet treatment lamps in the physiotherapy department. Nosy and noisy Yankee medical students breathing over my sterile dressings. And Samuel. Samuel was a racist charge nurse—we never hit it off. I always said to friends that one day I would get struck off the Nurses' Register for hanging a fellow member of staff, and it would probably be Samuel that got hung.

Now that was just the staff. The patients were in a class all their very own, with unnerving tendencies to drop off suddenly with things such as cardiac arrests—six the first week I was there, once when I was doing the donkey work for the physiotherapist. "Pat," she said, "I think your patient has arrested." Chaos ensued while other staff resuscitated the patient, leaving me standing alone.

Many patients were on ventilators, or "life-support machines" to the laymen. To me, these patients illustrated the concept of suffering. Imagine trying to allow a machine to push air into your lungs instead of inhaling normally. Imagine being sedated or, worse still, paralyzed with drugs to stop you from fighting the action of the machine. Imagine not being able to communicate.

I found it very stressful at first, especially with Samuel clattering around the unit like a mad puppet in his operating theater clogs, breathing over my shoulder like a leopard. Samuel is one odd guy. Never puts himself out to help the female nurses. He thinks women are limited by children, pregnancy, and menstruation. He once said to a group of us, "To me, pregnancy is like constipation." How he should know what pregnancy is like is beyond me. The surgical dressings room is a sort of lion's den where Samuel presides. His favorite trick is to call you into it to give you a telling off. I grew to dread his call: "Patricia, into the dressings room please." It happened many times.

I became more confident after a while, though, and I gained some respect in the unit when, on the night shift, I discovered arterial bleeding from a tracheostomy wound. The surgeon was raging when I beeped him the first time and wouldn't come down. The second time I thought he was going to kill me, but when he eventually came down and examined the wound, the throbbing and spurting you get from arterial bleeding was really obvious. My persistence in getting the lazy sot up probably saved

the lady's life, because she was whipped down to theater imme-
diately. Everyone was impressed, even the doctors. Only Samuel
could not bring himself to offer any praise.

One late shift, I got a new patient to look after. Mr. Turner
was an enormous man with a huge gut and covered with tattoos.
He was luminously yellow because of liver failure, due to the
drink, I suppose. He was a difficult man to nurse, as it required
four nurses to lift him or turn him to change his sheets or wash
his back. And the unit, like everywhere, was seriously short
staffed. It was a hard struggle to stop him from pulling his vari-
ous tubes out when his sedation wore off. Sometimes the seda-
tion would wear off but not the paralysant, and of course he
would still be unable to move. Then his blood pressure would
shoot sky high and his eyes would almost pop out of his head
with panic. I would feel like crying when I saw him like that.
Him being in that state meant that we had got it wrong, and that
worried me—one day my mam or me could be the patient, and
who would be there to make sure THEY got it right?

His first name was Jim. He had a very plain and dowdy wife
called Edie. She came every day with his grown-up sons, and she
would sit and hold his hand, stroking his forearm.

On Sundays, his mother would come, sit at his bed, and
stroke his forearm as well. I would watch from the nurses' sta-
tion and wonder if Jim felt irritated by those small, ticklish,
repetitive movements. Perhaps he would have liked Edie to
brave the tubing and kiss his forehead or caress his cheek. But I
could not suggest it, and Edie never did it. Sometimes his mate
would come in, covered in plaster dust, the dirty highlights in
his hair just hiding the gray, and wearing a gold earring. He
would sit and tell Jim all about the jobs he was finishing for him,
but Jim could not show any response.

Then I had a week out with bronchitis, and when I got back I
was allocated a "light patient," a nine-day post–heart attack, by
June, the nicest sister in the unit. Samuel had suggested I take
Jim again, but June could see that I'd come back to work sooner
than I should have and was kind to me. So in the evening, my
friend Lena and I were watching the patients and the show
"Eastenders" on the TV at my patient's bedside while the other
nurses were on their break. Lena asked me if I knew that Jim had
a fancy woman. I wasn't really interested since I was engrossed

in what Sharon and Grant were doing. In Ireland they haven't got "Eastenders," and in my part of Wexford our house couldn't get the cable for the English channels for years, so I just grunted at Lena.

"Oh yes," she went on, "she came in last night, only a few minutes after the wife went home. His friend brought her in. She's been here before." I wasn't interested in gossip, so I didn't give it much thought, but a few days later on the late shift, at a quarter to eight, the Fancy Woman came in again with Jim's mate, just as Edie had gone home. And from across the unit, as I folded up a sheet, I saw her. It was Doreen. Darren's mother, of all people! Now she was wearing a pair of earrings and her hair was permed, but she was as pale and gaunt as when I last saw her, and she was still wearing that sheepskin coat. So this was the Fancy Woman.

She came in and sat at the foot of the bed, but she never touched him. I went over to get something out of the cupboard and sneaked a look at her face. After a few minutes, she left, without looking at me or the other nurses.

A few days later I heard the wife and the mate rowing in the waiting room. She was screaming at him, "Les, how could you do it?" and he was saying sorry, but in the end, Edie collapsed in tears and June came out of the sisters' office to comfort her, the mate went out, and I ended up making the tea. After that, Doreen never again appeared in the unit, nor did the mate. The strain of Jim's illness was telling on Edie and the sons. I could not help thinking that the last thing they needed was Jim's mistress flaunting herself in the unit, but maybe that was none of my business. Edie got thinner and more haggard looking, and one day one of the sons, a strapping six footer with his father's beer gut, cried at his father's bed. The other son arrived on the unit drunk one night after the pubs had shut. I was on nights and persuaded the nurse-in-charge not to call security. I made him coffee in the kitchen.

He said he thought we nurses did a marvelous job, and he thought Ireland looked like a wonderful place for a holiday. He also asked me if I drank at the *Rose and Crown.* As I put his coffee on the table, he took my hand. "When will the old man come off life support, love?" I said I honestly didn't know.

"He's as tough as old boots. He'll make it." He squeezed my hand. I smiled and squeezed his hand back. All I could do.

A couple of weeks later I was on the early shift; the day had started badly. I was late for work because of the traffic. And Samuel swooped. In the Lion's Den he proclaimed that I was not professional enough to be a nurse — and was I spending too much time in the social club? For once I stood up for myself and asked him to stop picking on me. It was the first time I had ever been late. Then I said that he had been very unsupportive as a senior nurse and had made it very hard for me to fit in. He said he would have to see the director of nursing about my attitude, and I said OK, I would be speaking to the director of nursing as well. Then I walked out, slamming the door, and disappeared into the toilets.

I spoke to the NUPE rep, who said to see the director of nursing as soon as possible. But, as luck would have it, she was not available. I left a message with her secretary and spent the rest of the day avoiding Samuel.

In the afternoon, I was washing out the bedpans in the sluice room when June came running in. "Pat, you're not afraid of spiders, are you?"

"No, why?"

"Because there is a monster crawling around the unit. Can you come and get him please?"

The monster was terrorizing Lena in the middle of the floor, while the conscious patients were watching the flapping nurses gleefully from their beds. I picked up a tissue paper from a box at the nurses' station and bent down, trying to coax the spider on it so that I could let it out through the window.

Suddenly, from the entrance to the unit came the shrill voice of Samuel and the demented clicking of those clogs as he clattered across. "What are you doing, stupid girl!" and with that he stamped. Splat! The spider was crushed.

I looked around at four coronary patients gazing at Samuel in despair. They were supposed to have peace and quiet. Not the mad puppet. And not me either, because I snapped. A day of worrying about my job and a dead spider made me lose control. I screamed, "You evil bastard!" at him. There was no need to do that to the poor spider. I said he must be nuts. And all the time

Samuel was chanting *vermin, vermin* (about the spider I think, not me) and telling me I was going to be severely disciplined, if not struck off, if he could help it. I'm afraid I told him that he was the biggest arshole I ever had to work with, just as the director of nursing walked into the unit to see me.

Then, the student looking after Jim Turner let out a yell. "He's arrested, he's arrested!" as the cardiac monitor showed the desperate flailing of his heart. Everyone snapped into action, scrambling to his bed. Lena performed cardiac massage. The student nurse called the resuscitation team. I took over manually ventilating him with an air bag. June drew up the drugs into syringes. Samuel ran around like a headless chicken and "co-ordinated"—that was his job, and he did it well I must admit. Even the director reassured the other patients. We all tried. We really did.

But it was no good, and in the end Jim died. His wife was called. The student nurse and I performed Last Offices. We made him look the best we could. At least he was free of the tubes and needles now.

When Edie came in, she lay her head on his chest and cried. The student nurse wiped her eyes, and so did I. After a little while Edie kissed his poor limp mouth and whispered, "Good-bye my darling"; then she was led away by her sons. It was a quarter to five. Time for me to go home, but Samuel had not quite finished.

"You're to see the director of nursing tomorrow at nine-fifteen," he smirked. I nodded curtly as I walked into the kitchen where Shirley, the domestic, was having a cigarette. She threw one over to me. "His Fancy Woman was outside a little while ago. Poor cow. I feel sorry for her now. She works in Gerries, doesn't she?"

I felt very weary by then. I pulled off my cap and belt, shoved them both in my bag, and wandered out into the car park. But as I got to the car, I saw Doreen sitting on a bench in the grounds. So I went over.

"Hello. I'm very sorry about Jim," I said, cringing inwardly. Doreen just muttered, "I know. Thanks," and looked at the ground. I felt I had to say something else.

"I've met you before, haven't I?"

"Yeah, love. You went out with my Darren once, didn't you?"

"That's right. How is he?"

"Inside again. Chip off the old block really. His dad's inside as well."

I asked if I could give her a lift anywhere, but she shook her head. Then I asked her if she would be going to Jim's funeral.

"Oh no, I won't be doing that. The trouble that would cause. No, he's all hers now." She pulled her coat tightly around her. "Look, love, I appreciate your concern, but I'm all right. Off you go."

So I left her in solitary grief on the bench. As I drove to the exit of the hospital, I stopped at the zebra crossing to let a group of people cross. There was Edie Turner, cradled against one son's shoulder and followed by the other son. The family made their way out of the gates and across the road to the bus stop.

And me? I parked and went to join the queue of other nurses losing the battle against the weed. I was going to need a packet of fags. It's not every evening that you go home to compose a letter of resignation. Wexford is crying out for nurses. I'm going back.

Tourniquet

SHIRLEY KOBAR *Aurora, Colorado*

She showed her arms,
skin paper-thin
tiny blue streams
on a bruised map.
Cuddled them and rocked.
"They couldn't get it.
Here and here they tried,"
pointing to a diary of failure.
"Will they send someone else?"
"No, not today," I said
syringe and tourniquet buried
deep within my pocket.

Gift

SHIRLEY KOBAR *Aurora, Colorado*

The bottle is upended,
so my thirsty hands and spirit will
receive a dollop of your last gift;
when it is gone I will have a funeral again.

For a year I have thought of the days
of your dying and your dignity.
The reminder an everyday ritual
as simple and soothing as stroking
lotion on my skin.
I cared for you, and
for a year you have cared for me.
What nurse has never needed healing?

The Lullaby

JEANNE LEVASSEUR *Columbia, Connecticut*

You are holding the telephone
for a dying woman, right against her cheek,
a woman near coma for weeks, now
her throat opened for breathing
and unable to speak.

You think this call hopeless,
the waterwheels softening,
slowly easing their rush and flood.
Then she hears her daughter's voice,
her eyes dilate, and her face,

which looked puffy with drugs,
takes on that soft, smudgy light of May,
when women in mountain villages open their shutters
and the early air tumbles in, gauzy and pink.

I don't know what her daughter said,
but it's as if this woman were surveying the blue
alleys of the town below, mountains brightening
in the east. She cradles the phone,
makes clicking sounds with her tongue,
tapping excitedly with one finger,
the low drowning in her throat like reeds
rushing in streams.

What did her daughter understand?
I write this for her:

Your mother lay with the phone beside her ear.
Those sounds you heard were a lullaby.
You made all the difference.
She died rocking a baby to sleep.

Hospital Parking Garage

JEANNE LeVASSEUR *Columbia, Connecticut*

He is just my father's age
and her nightgown blazes in a paper bag,
an open grief of objects
marked property of Ida Jennings.

Who will hold him in the bluish glow of morning?
He climbs into an old gray car
and sets the paper bag carefully
on the seat beside him.

He has no talent for making up a life.
Flowered bedsheets surprise him.
Tonight he will have much to hear,
years ticking in every creak and sound.

His hands lie idle in his lap, then he turns
the key. Everywhere the world is disappearing.

Danny Boy

JEANNE LeVASSEUR *Columbia, Connecticut*

Your parents lean over you like aspen trees
and the hospital room becomes a grove.
Their hamper laid open with pickles and sausage,
all to tempt you into moving, speaking,
laughing again, your mouth full of sunlight.
To see this, your mother would chain herself to an oven
and feed it with splinters of her own bones.

Your father would exchange places with you
in the car that crashed, he would be your headlights
and go before you if he could.

They come everyday, sit and speak with you.
Your mother knits, your father reads the newspaper.
She has started at the cerebellum and the worsted trails
off her needle like a stem.
See the ball of gray yarn in her basket huddled like a brain.
She is knitting webs and crannies, *pia mater*, and hopes
your damaged mind, which flies around the room like swallows,
will come and nest again.
Your father reads out loud some clippings
you would have liked. He thinks if he reads enough,
he can change the course of history.
And you lie there, your heart valves slamming closed,

the message your body hears: Live, live!
This picnic is spread across your blanket.
They are waiting for the crows to shake themselves from trees,
or for something like sunlight on shards of glass
and the gleam from twisted chrome to knit itself into shade.
They are waiting for you to waken,
to take a peach in your open hand and remember
how good it is to eat.

Secrets

JEANNE LeVASSEUR *Columbia, Connecticut*

A braid of girls in white sleeves stood
around the woman who was being fixed
with clicking chemicals wedged in straws.
All to be inserted above the elbow,
just where a man might grab and shake her,
if he were angry. And her little girl sitting
on a stool in the corner of the room,
watching, feeling nauseous.

I overheard, "There won't be no more
like you at home." And we weren't girls,
we were women watching a new procedure.
How the straws could be inserted so the woman didn't feel.
The numbing needle going first and then the cylinder
with its barrel full of thin white straws levering under skin.

Everything went flawlessly, the incision was no bigger
than the tiny scar on her daughter's knee.
Near the end, she raised her hand to wave to her little girl,
so quiet and dizzy on her stool.
And I liked her better for remembering the girl,
pale and underfed, who looked as if she had twirled
too long on a carousel.

But she didn't really wave. I only wished
she did, wished the woman had lifted her hand
with the rose tattoo, made some motion
to the white-faced little girl.

When the girl got sick, her mother slapped her
and I forgot this too, feeling dizzy and remote,
busy helping them on with their coats.

I remember them leaving in matching scarves and mittens.
Did I really hear her whisper, *Sometimes mommy hurts me.*

Wasn't I just a girl gripping white sleeves across my chest,
was there something I was supposed to do?

What Abel Says

PATRICIA MAHER *Brookline, Massachusetts*

Abel talks in stories.
He tells me a string of them
about the sea
and a small boat anchored
yet moving with the wind and water.
Abel tells me
he too is anchored
anchored to his house
by the dirt, he says.
I listen, realizing my silence
is the precious thing I bring.
It makes a space for hope.

My breathing is shallow
the stench is so deep
at Abel's.
My foot stamps
to keep the gray mice away
his pets, he says
since he lost his dog.
He eats cold beans out of the can
happy for my company.

Frayed shirt and long beard
his shoes are molded to his feet.
I took them off for him once
but now we just
stand facing his mantle
and look at the pictures and bills.
His wife's pocketbook
although she's long gone

sits open
as if she might return
like an anchor
he can't bear to pull up
nor can I, yet.

God and the Telephone

VENETA MASSON *Washington, D.C.*

Why don't you come
when I phone?

> *I come once a week —*
> *sometimes more.*
> *Somedays you're*
> *calling me every*
> *few minutes. How*
> *can I come every time?*

When I call you
it's always important.
Last night I slid
out of my chair
and had to sit there
on the floor for hours.

> *It couldn't have been*
> *quite as bad as you say*
> *because when you phoned*
> *for me to come*
> *what you asked for*
> *was chicken and ice cream.*

Well, I have to think
about Lady Jane Jackson!
You're young and
you have your strength.
You have to come.

> *But phone calls every day*
> *and all night long?*

Well, if you can't
be called, you ain't
gonna hold a job for long.
You don't have
that many patients.

       Do you know when you call
       you always yell
       and say I have to
       come right away?

I don't want to hear —
Who yells?
Look here Sweetheart.
There are only two things
Lady Jane needs —
God and this pink telephone.
But God is a spirit
and sometimes I need
a flesh and blood person.
That's you.

Pouring It Down

VENETA MASSON *Washington, D.C.*

Sweetheart, will you take
this little pan
to the bathroom
and pour it down the john.
Pour it down the john, hear
don't pour it nowhere but
down the john, okay?

> *I'll pour it down the john.*

Don't pour it in the sink now
'cause it's acting up in there
something ridiculous —

> *I'll pour it down the john.*

— and don't pour it down the tub
'cause the tub's stopped up
and you can see I have
enough trouble as it is.
Just pour it down the john.

> *I poured it down the john.*

And why are these legs
backfiring on me?
Why are they acting like this?

> *Because they're swollen up.*

All this water comin' between
the bone and the skin
makin' it sag and seep.

I thought they were just gonna
heal themselves up
inside a couple of days.

> *See, as long as you sit*
> *in that chair night and day*
> *your legs are going to stay*
> *swollen, and as long*
> *as they're swollen*
> *they're going to seep —*

Ouch! That's so tender.
Stop! I can't stand that.

> *— and now I'm concerned*
> *because there are open sores*
> *where the blisters were.*

Never mind that.
Just take this pan
to the bathroom
and pour it
down the john.
Don't pour it down
the sink, mind.
Don't pour it nowhere
but down the john.

Snowbound

VENETA MASSON *Washington, D.C.*

So we are homebound
in a snowbound city
where only "essential" employees
reported to work.

Surely *we* are essential,
or at least *I* am,
to one or two if not to all.

> To Sadie perhaps
> or Sultana or Nellie
> Alma
> Alberta
> or Herman.

> Invalids, they are homebound
> not just today but all year round.

Who will dress their wounds if not we?
Who will bring them their pills?
Who will hear their frail hearts
        and scarred lungs
        and night fears
        if not we — or me?

But we are snowbound.
On the telephone
we agonize over the fact
that we're frozen in place.

Surely it is essential
to get to them, isn't it?
to one or two if not to all?

Yet all have survived
except Herman who died
quietly
this morning
in his chair.

The Arithmetic of Nurses

VENETA MASSON *Washington, D.C.*

S-s-s, S-s-s, S-s-s
Bennie Smith is trying to speak.
I am counting out cookies
from a faded blue tin.

S-s-s, S-s-s, S-s-s
Twelve!
Are twelve cookies enough to hold
a sick old man for thirty-six hours?
Twelve cookies and one can of juice?
Twelve cookies wrapped in a towel
tucked under a pillow where roaches
ply a brisk trade in crumbs?

Six!
He blurts it out
face lit up by the restless flicker
of the television screen.
No, twelve, I muse.
Unless someone comes
that's all he'll have
till I get back again.

S-s-s-six thousand!
He strains under the weight of the words.
Clearly he has something important to say
but I am caught up with my own calculations —

The number of minutes
it will take a rivulet of urine
to reach the screaming bedsores
on his back

The number of degrees
his temperature will rise
as infection sets in

The number of days
it will take him
to let me call the ambulance

The number of times
I must walk the long hall
to this dim little room
the width of a bed.

His stiff body straddles the low bed
like a piece of plywood on a sawhorse.
Push down on the feet, up comes the head.
I tilt my ear toward his mouth
to catch the stutterings

S-s-s-six thousand nurses . . .
on strike today . . .
Meh- Meh- Meh- Minnesota!

Half his face breaks into a grin
for if there's one thing Bennie understands
it's the arithmetic of nurses
and old, abandoned men.

Litany of Dolores

VENETA MASSON *Washington, D.C.*

Ay, qué bonita viene.

> Chimes from the church across the street
> mark the hours of my visits, chime ten
> or two or four as I climb the dark stairs
> pull open the knobless door of the room
> where you lie like a broken doll
> waiting for me as if for the fresh-faced child
> who may forget to come, having so many
> other, more precious possessions.

Que Dios le bendiga, Dios le pague.

> God will repay the small mercies I offer —
> hot coffee, an ear to receive your confessions
> aspirin, bandages, pair after pair of shoes
> you can't wear because of the fire
> that is melting your joints.
> And yet you, too, are a giver of gifts —
> creams and perfumes by Estée Lauder
> strings of beads from the toe of a stocking
> a black paper fan you got from your sister
> Revlon's Finest Professional Emery Boards.

Viera como me duele.

> You left your country, your mother's house
> to help your sister raise her infant son
> and the shock of her death ignited a fire
> deep in your bones. Marcos, too, is consumed
> with bitterness. Looking at you, he rails
> at the God who took his wife.
> You could have had *her!* he cries.
> Why did you not take *her* instead?

Todo lo malo que hace se paga.

> The fire inside flashes up in your eyes
> and your chin juts out when you speak
> of the evils that Marcos has done
> in the time since Lydia died.
> He won't let you turn on the heat or light
> took away the TV set, brings you nothing
> but rice at the end of the day, though he fixes
> frijoles and meat for himself. Worst of all
> he's set the child against you, encouraged him
> in petty cruelties — laughed when he marked up
> your body with crayons. Yes, God will repay
> the evils of Marcos. All he's done will be repaid.

Perdone que le moleste.

> Forgive me, you say, for talking like this
> and pardon me for bothering you, but hand me
> my stick with the nail on the end
> a threaded needle to mend this sweater
> I think there is a clean towel in that bag
> some medicine for the pain, perhaps
> a spray of cologne behind my ears
> and pardon me, pardon me, pardon me.

Quiero caminar. Voy a caminar!

> There were days when you spoke of walking again
> and days in summer when hope hung sweet
> and ripe as the mangoes of home. You stood
> gripping the rails of your walker, inching through
> the doors toward the stairs that led
> to the kitchen. One day I will be happy, you said
> but by the time you reached the third step
> your strength was gone. No more, you said, no more.

Quiero que sea conmigo cuando yo muero.

I have closed your eyes, washed away
the burning heat of your fever, laid you out
in the lavender gown, hung the necklace
I brought from Copán around your neck.
The child and I sit side by side
drinking the sodas I sent him to buy
paging the album you asked me to hide.
There are pictures of women and children and seasons.
We look at the book and talk of your life
and stop when we reach the blank pages.

Night Walker

LIANNE ELIZABETH MERCER *Fredericksburg, Texas*

I click the lock of the psychiatric intensive care unit, leave restless minds and sad hands behind, slip into the black cat night. Inside the building, I am the supervisor. Outside, no one knows my name. I become a tree, listen for sounds of footsteps. Possums invade the civilized dreams of sidewalks. The security guard talks on the radio to the PBX operator. Indifferent gray grass hides the small wars of scorpions and roaches. A mockingbird sings an elusive song to souls stalking hope. The night licks its fur and yawns, but its eyes never close.

Empty Swing

LIANNE ELIZABETH MERCER *Fredericksburg, Texas*

You still the swing,
no flowers, still, no voices,
no wind. Mountains crack you
from your egg, conjure clouds,
rain your conversations
until you burst.
Rocks too heavy to carry
tumble from your eyes.

You abandon your arms, choose
the small, locked room, hang your head,
huddle on the bare mattress
inside this kind, pink skin.
We stay beside you,
faceless curtain of hair,
window without sky. Still,
you pee on the floor,
scratch holes in your wrists,
spit your blood at us, scream
when we give you soap and Ativan.

Walls crack. Words drown in a downpour.
Your hands grab empty voices, cannot stay
still. Secret flower, you
hug your knees, beg us to lock the door
again. We grow weary
calling your name, fragile
orchid sinking in still wind.

Bea's Last Vacation

MURIEL MURCH *Bolinas, California*

It's just a tonsillectomy
she'll be home tomorrow
no big deal, even though
it's harder when they're older.
   Bigger tonsils — more manipulation.
   Cavernous crypts — more pain.
   Larger vessels — more blood.
and
it's my baby they're talking about,
   I'm her mother.

They're in awe of her, a TEENAGER in Pediatrics,
but in nineteen-seventy-three you could hold all
four pounds of her in one hand.
A living translucent doll
with the heart of a hunted panther
and the courage of a virgin queen
and . . . that was all.

They took her in there —
through those heavy, thick swinging doors —
you can't go in there if you know your place.
I know my place, I'm her mother.

Are they careful with her body?
Not everyone thinks she's beautiful.
I do, I'm her mother.

Are they competent,
careful of their reputation?
Or are they artists,
confident enough to combine wisdom with knowledge?
I want to go in. I'm her mother.

She's breathing, steady and deep,
morphine and oxygen glide through the streams of her body.
I would bend over sideways to catch
   quick-little-baby-breaths
when I was first — her mother.

She is a woman now
California skin, long hair, regular menses.
   Where did you get those breasts child?
Home from high school, NO MORE EXAMS!
Only honors classes to finish in glory,
and colleges to choose from.
Your mind reaches outward and forward
To Tesla, and East, and Crew, and Europe, and Max and . . .
   it's *your* mind.

I sit here and watch you, writing my love for you.
This week I will care for you,
fuss over and enjoy you,
then you will go,
   and I will stay.
I know my place,
   I am your mother.

    April 1991
    All my love, mum.

From Journey in the Middle of the Road

MURIEL MURCH *Bolinas, California*

Blackberry Farm
Summer 1989
Dearest Uncle,

Where am I? I park as far away as I comfortably can, need-
ing the time to adjust my mind as I walk up the aisle of 19th Ave.
into this cold new world. Angular gray slabs with cutting straight
seams rise out of a summer bed of perpetual fog. Within the
State University classrooms, the fluorescent overhead lights are
always on.

As an acknowledgment to working students, our classes start
in the afternoon. First a lecture, followed by a period in the lab.
Sixty of us have been divided into two groups, each with its own
teacher. Priscilla is an older, petite lady, elegantly permed and
suited, yet glinting beneath her hose is a gold ankle bracelet.
Among the pictures hanging in the corridor, I spot her face in
the class of 1974. Even then as an older student, her eyes twinkle,
prompting my curiosity about her story. Betsy is younger, softer
yet grayer, and at first seems too gentle for our group, which sits
waiting, on the edge of belligerence.

Each class is a mixture of older, diploma nurses, some from
the army, and a couple of new graduates from the two-year pro-
grams. There are a few licensed vocational nurses and a strange as-
sortment of college graduates, mostly from other health-related
fields. As older RNs, we can't help but stare at these "civilians"
in wonder at their choosing to become nurses. Have they seen
us somewhere making a difference? Have they sensed the ful-
fillment that we ourselves often grow immune to?

The content of this month's course is insulting to some
nurses and incomprehensible to others, so I guess it is a good
leveler. Patiently guided by Priscilla and Betsy, we are brought
together as a group. With increasing mutual respect for our
mixed backgrounds and individual commitment to this path, we
begin to acknowledge each other. The concept of nursing diag-

nosis is very familiar to the young nurses, but I am among those who have never heard of it before. I am instinctively suspicious that this has more to do with a misguided bid for professionalism (a word we hear far too much of here) and covering the proverbial arse than with really improving patient care.

Other teachers from the department come into the class and present their specialties. Unwittingly, I discover I have become an "attitude problem" for one teacher. She returns my assignment with an incomprehensibly low grade of 27 out of 50. I find myself spitting with frustration and fury but am saved by two of the "we've been here before" savvy Master's students. "Now Aggie, this is what you do. . . ." I ask for and am granted a second opportunity to right my wrongs and redo the paper. Taking a chance, I rewrite the entire thing verbatim, changing only four lines. The grade goes from 27 to 47, and again I learn the reality of personality over professionalism (that word again). I don't know when I've been more angry, after the first grade or the second.

I have not yet found the sweetener for the bitter taste of my cynicism. There is a palpable restlessness in all of us when they keep banging on about the "type" of nurse and the "quality" of patient care. The male nurses tighten their lips when this talk comes up. The intangible qualities and drive that brought us all here go purposely unrecognized. We must relearn our place as students. If we felt acknowledged as the nurses we believe we are, we could go forward with less caution.

What a kvetch. I should be, and am, so excited about being here, and yet I feel unsteady and unsure of what it is that disturbs me. A strange muddle for the mind. I have a month off after this block, then another month of classes before joining the mainstream in the fall. A small breather to catch up with the family.

Bless you for being there, where?

Your Aggie.

Blackberry Farm
October 20, 1989
Oh Harold,

There is a lone bee flying around up here in my room. She goes from color to color, from frustration to frantic as she looks for something, anything, to be a real flower. That is how I feel in this city's university. I climb the dark back stairs of the science building to the overbright second-floor corridor. The first few engineering classes keep their doors open, and, peeking in, I see their intense community. Beyond them the nursing labs and nursing faculty offices are marked by their cryptic and austere closure. I walk quickly and carefully, always aware of how my feet touch the ground. Each day, I reclaim my right to be here.

All the classes this semester are nursing classes. I am still looking for a topic for a worthwhile nursing research project—something that has made a real contribution to the quality of nursing care and is cost effective. I know there must be some out there, but they remain elusive. So far I have read through reams of wasted time and effort by people who should know better. To top it off, this class is taught in monotony, suitable for the mechanical skills of a ten year old.

Pathophysiology clocks in for a measly two units and yet consumes every unclaimed moment. In the lecture hall each tiny seat is overflowing with student, bag, books, lunch, and tape recorder. But nobody eats lunch during this lecture. We pay rapt attention while Kay, dynamic and expensively elegant, hones her course content to a fifty-minute perfection. We vie for front seats, straining for more absorption. In awe, I told Waltersun there were at least a hundred and fifty in the class. He looked at me with mock compassion while he said, "Mum, there are over four hundred in my anthro class." What do I know? Not very much, it seems. I studied harder and deeper than I ever had from the textbooks, only to find that all the questions were taken from the syllabus. The questions are convoluted and confusing; I follow what seems to be three or four logical steps forward and then lose it on the last part. I have just scraped through one test and failed another. I am in awe of the many minds that score so well here and am beginning to believe that they really are smarter than I am.

The lab sections are smaller and taught by different instructors. The content is insufficient for nurses who have little practical knowledge of technique and demeaning for those who do this daily. Many of our group try to get out of the lab but I am not successful. We help each other, and in this class I find myself a better teacher than student, and I wonder at my arrogance.

Community health is also team-taught in two classes. The teachers obviously enjoy and respect each other, and we are refreshed by this camaraderie. In the main lecture section it is easy to spot those nurses who have smelled the fetid underbelly of disease in the world, as opposed to those young students who are terrified of the anger of life and death found away from the hospital bedside. One teacher's soft form belies a sharp mind. I think it is his frustration with the academic hierarchy that has produced the easing of his belt line.

The other teacher is responsible for guiding us through our community clinical rotation. I have chosen to work with a residential center/school for young boys in trouble that was started on the outskirts of our village nearly twenty years ago. Despite the community's reputation for acceptance and free culture, there was a lot of hostility toward the school. Inching its way forward, the program now has two residential sites, a reunification program, and a high-school support program. They have only recently received funding, and hired a nurse. It's just my cup of tea. Half of the kids haven't had physicals, and of those that have, half haven't followed up on the recommendations. Immunizations are a casual affair and medical care just leapfrogs from one crisis to another.

The kids are mostly outrageously inappropriate, coming at me constantly with little things, checking out how seriously I will take them, how much naughtiness and cuddling can they get away with. Lots, is the answer. I am happy to let them come to me thinking they have gotten away with something. I slowly go about my business, staying steady and sure enough so they can eventually go about theirs. Slowly, like young colts, they come quietly and feel safe now. The older boys check me out and, if it suits them, connect. If not, they just watch. The young ones bounce and giggle, still not sure where I really fit in or if I will stay around, a big issue in their lives. I laugh at myself as I firmly close a door on one set of teenage responsibilities only to open the door on another. Who is trying to tell me what, I wonder?

End of time, never the end of my love.

Aggie

The City
April 18, 1990
Dear Uncle Harold,

Today is a quiet time of reflection and absorption before the immediate NOW returns. Yesterday held a new adventure as I found my way across Market Street and down to San Francisco General Hospital by eleven A.M. sharp.

Working the system, I have set up next semester's clinical to learn what I want to learn, while diplomatically appearing to use something called "Nursing Process." It took two busses before the number nine, like a full garbage truck, spat me and some more of the city's refuse out on the sidewalk in front of the hospital. My heart lifted when I saw the big old red-brick complex standing stoically on the street, hiding its new concrete blocks up the back alleys. It reminded me so much of my old training hospital that I knew I had come home.

Turning through the doorway of the women's clinic, I was thrust into a swarm of multiracial confusion and frustration. The faces of patients and staff alike were sullen and beaten, at best resigned. I breathed in the stale air purposely, and calmly smiled into the faces at the information desk, where the openness of my smile seemed like the surprise of their day. That openness will have to be one of my gifts to the clinic—if they are to look at me as anything other than another burden in the shape of an out-of-touch old returnee student nurse they have to carry around for sixteen weeks. The nurse in charge of the teen clinic is a thin angular woman, not yet softened by a lover's touch. The fact that I am old enough to be her mother I consider awesome and she considers despicable. I found myself asking naive clinical questions I should know the answers to. It turns out that more than half the patients at teen clinic come from South America and speak primarily Spanish. So my next stop is a big medical library to find Spanish tapes I can play all summer in the car. I'm not sure what I am walking into at San Francisco General, but I know I will come out of it being more aware of what it is like to be young, poor, and pregnant in a big city.

Later in the Student Union, I met up with our group from Speech and Communication. I feel far too old to be put through something as corny as a "group presentation," but I have to shed my age and embarrassment and turn that around, which I do by being fascinated by the research. Patti with her short permed black hair is the youngest of Chinese twenty year olds, working hard at her family restaurant and going to school full time. Shareene's soft brown skin glows, and with her perfect teeth, long golden brown hair, and frills under her shorts is the most gorgeous of San Francisco mixes, shining with an inner light that suffuses her natural physical beauty. We picked censorship as our project, and the first assignment was to go see the Maplethorpe exhibition in Berkeley. From the gates of the museum through the halls, it was packed to shuffling with people eager to have "seen" this work. Nobody in the photographs or the museum was smiling or laughing for the joy of living. Looking at one photo of a faceless black male nude, I was struck not only by the beauty of his form but by the fear in his heart. The portraits of the children reminded me of myself as a child, budding with an as yet unnamed sadness. I looked at the faces of these two young souls I had brought with me, so very different in outlook and style, and wondered what they saw as they carried their own natural fears of being twenty and at the very beginning of it all.

This morning San Francisco was awakened by quite a strong earthquake. The city paused, the last quake being too close in our memories for urban bravado. After it stopped I took a walk on Sutter Street to find the swimming pool. Half an hour later there it was, not huge but certainly lapable and affordable. Later I walked back on Post, feeling airy and tingly everywhere, the memory of the water still on my skin. I was brought back to the street by the sweetest of voices. "Is this straight?" A slight brown man was holding a flagpole up outside an apartment building, and, after figuring out the straightness of the pole, we got chatting. Harlen told me he is from the Bahamas. Six months ago he had an English girlfriend. "The best woman I ever had, but her mother got sick and she had to go home and cannot come back."

His heart is broken but not his spirit, and he was delighted to speak to someone else from England.

He said he was 49, so I told him I was 47. He didn't believe it. "I have four children," I said, thinking this would help convince him. "And a husband?" he asked quickly. I paused as I realized my truth. "I don't know." We talked a minute or two longer before returning to our own lives, each carrying the gift of the other.

Life is this. Moments to see and feel. To walk into the chaos of humanity at the hospital and later pause at the beauty of rhododendrons in the park. To meet a new friend at eight in the morning and wonder if I hadn't just been touched by an angel. Goodness and love still flow through the human spirit and I run with joy to share and embrace it all.

Love to you, wherever you are.

Aggie.

Blackberry Farm
October 2, 1990
Dearest Vibika,

Here are more naked ladies to bloom in the depths of Denmark. They like to be crowded together and often take two years before they settle in, feel comfortable, and flower.

Our vacation came and went, you phoned, and time rushes on. It is now October with autumn sunshine and heat that fools no one. There is a new crop of monarch butterflies in the eucalyptus grove about our house. They are resting for a few days before continuing south. It takes ten generations to make the trip to Mexico and back!

School has started again, and even with a clinical it is not as frantic as the last two semesters. I am working at San Francisco General Hospital in the women's clinic, primarily with pregnant teenagers. Part of me feels I have awakened and come home. I stay in the city and take the bus to the "other" side of town. As I crossed the road to the bus stop on my first morning, I looked up to see two men. The younger one, standing behind his older companion, started to vomit and tried to move toward the gutter. What has died in me, that the instinct to put my arm around him and help him was stilled the second it rose? I really did pull my jacket tighter as I walked away from them and deeper into my own life.

My friend Philomina had been at the hospital since seven-thirty. What we found was no charge nurse, and none of the other nurses knowing or wanting to know that we were there. The clinic is desperately overworked and understaffed. Employees look at us more as students who will *be* work rather than as RNs who can work. Changing this would require more clinical efficiency than I feel I possess at this point. The quantity of charting has me overwhelmed as I remember — or worse, forget — all the tests that are required. I feel so deeply incompetent at times that I just want to weep, especially when I remember that I really was a good hospital nurse. Slowly it makes more sense, however, and I am able to do better. The patients are a wonderful mix of Latinas, Asians, and Afro-Americans, with a few Europeans, Arabs, and inner-city whites. Their common denominator is poverty and an unsureness of their place in society, never mind in this clinic. Many don't speak English, and although I am learning some Spanish, I often have to work with an interpreter. I also use the fact that I am English and not American. Many of the patients take on the role of hostess or teacher, although I am asking the questions.

Last week the clinics were so busy that I got to help out with the regular drop-in clinic. I call it "drop in and hang out." Sometimes it can take several hours from registration at the front desk to getting through the nurses' station, before spending more time waiting for a young frazzled intern. This is a teaching hospital, and, although the interns learn a lot of science, there is no room here to pause and feel a patient's fear, to look that patient in the eye and give her an honest smile of caring. On this day I found an eighty-five-year-old woman sitting in dignified upright silence for at least two hours in the waiting room. She was accompanied by two sisters from her community who waited while I led her to the examination room. As I bent over her, I could smell the musty perfume of stale air that came from her clothes. Locked windows and her unsteady balance have precluded her walking alone in her neighborhood. Precariously seated on the table, she demurely stated she was here because of vaginal bleeding and, as an aside, said her breasts were very tender. I quietly asked her if she would show me, and as my hands gently touched her breasts and I felt the too familiar nodular hardness, a chill enveloped my body. Right there I prayed that these eager young doctors would not get so involved with a diagnosis of cancer that they would forget her as a woman.

As you can see, I am quite caught up in it, which is just as well because I need to be. Luckily, the rest of the family is too busy to notice. Walter is editing, Carrie is on tour, Connie is working, Waltersun and Bea are at school.

That's about it for now, dear. I knew I wouldn't do a stroke of homework today until after I had written this letter.

Yours as ever,
Aggie

Blackberry Farm
October 15, 1990
Dear Uncle Harold,

The week begins promptly at seven-thirty this morning with a chainsaw relentlessly whining in the background to remind me of how much work there is always to be done. "Eight," with feline presumption, is sitting behind my desk. The morning sun is on his back as he faces me with one forearm draped across the keyboard, staring unblinkingly at his own view of the typewriter.

This whole semester is about communication. The one class I am really having trouble with is Critical Thinking. It is infinitely confusing, and although I find it harder than anyone else, some of the other kids are struggling too. It cannot be easy to teach, either. In Holistic Health, George's new agenda is "text" and postmodernist thought. I haven't even gotten to modernist yet. He is slower than molasses, but very thorough. Although I don't and won't believe that language, as it is defined, is the criteria for humanity, his path is always interesting. Somewhere here there is an argument for the bonding of nurses and doctors, but not of teachers, that is related to language—but I cannot grasp and articulate it yet.

Daily my passion grows for clinical at General. I have learned my first word of Korean: *Aggie*, it means baby! A young couple came in accompanied by their own interpreter. She had just managed to get to America to join her husband a week before her due date. We spent the entire morning together. They spoke, the interpreter listened, and I listened. I spoke, the interpreter listened, they listened, and he meticulously covered sheets of paper in small, neat Korean. What an adventure life is. I wish them luck.

Through persistence and motherly nagging, the attendance at the teen clinic is up! I am unashamedly proud of that. One young lady not only showed up for the second time, but she was clean and bright-eyed when she did. I have promised that every time she comes to clinic, I will find half an hour to work with her alone on some aspect of childbirth preparation. I have prepared a syllabus of childbirth education classes for this teenage population, quite different from what I taught to the motivated young mothers of the late sixties, seventies, and eighties. The classes are given in both English and Spanish, but even that does not help everybody.

I teach these classes pushing through my anger, childishly yearning for a just God. I try to explain the incredible changes going on in their bodies because of pregnancy and impending labor when they have not yet accepted the changes of adolescence. Sometimes we scrap it all, and they talk about school, life, home, and how to survive on the streets. All I can really give them is acceptance, some understanding and confidence. Getting through high school is a major goal. They have a chance if they can do that.

The teens' parents show up as infrequently as the boyfriends. The boyfriends slide in shyly, embarrassed and confused but not a little proud and curious about this world so concerned with their creation. The parents are nearly always angry and on guard, at every turn expecting a judgment on their own parenting. Mother and soon-to-be mother parry in hostile defense, the anger that binds them like turning taffy. One grandmother drives a hundred miles to San Francisco every two weeks to bring in her granddaughter who could not make it across town without her. While I am afraid for the lightning-quick starved body with taut skin and unseeing eyes that carries another hungry infant, I give thanks for the awesome strength of the resilient, brittle old black woman who is already loving this unborn child.

Time to move back into another world. Back to the dentist, then off to school and another lovely test tonight. Two envelopes crammed with graduate school applications have arrived and lie intimidatingly on the kitchen table. Even if I have the ability to fill them out, I can't believe that I would get accepted to either school, so will just write and write. I can't seem to stop anyway. OK, here I go again, supported by your love, strength, and care.

Aggie.

White Flame before the Long Black Wall

MADELEINE MYSKO *Lutherville, Maryland*

Miles from this wakefulness, the long black wall keeps naming
   the dead,
Vowels and consonants glimmering in the moonlight, a roll call
   the stars read.

Shall I leave the solid yellow of this kitchen,
The air pure with the sleep of my children,
The comfort of this table with its bowl of fruit?
Shall I go to the long black wall
And press their names into my hands?

What are their names?

I have lost their names,
And lost their stories —
Left them the other end
Of twenty-five years.

What of remembrance
That distant window?

Window gleaming in the white-hot sun —
Texas, August 1969.
The ledge white-on-white —
Pigeon droppings here and there.
And the pigeons — gray — seem to fly white
Into the waiting air.

The patients arrive glistening white,
Stripped and slathered with sulfanilamide,
Their privates draped in cloths — small, white —
And the freshest burn is thickly white,
And sheets lie long and flatly white
Where a leg or arm is gone.

O Death wears white
In this hard white frame,
And bides his time
With the fires of Vietnam.

The room beyond the window
Flares again and again and again:
Now a marine,
Aged seventeen,
Brown eyes,
One arm, no legs, flesh cut away,
Swirls of blood in the dead-white tub.
He cries.
He cries my name.

Nurse.

I watch him burning down — *white flame* —
White flame before the long black wall that keeps naming,
    naming the dead.

Wisteria

LESLIE NYMAN *Pelham, Massachusetts*

A shudder of resistance shivered through me as I ran toward the old brick hospital. November's icy rain had stripped the last of the wisteria from the vines covering the stone-gray building. In spring, when I began my nursing career, the smell of these purple flowers filled the air; now the chill dampness of late autumn drained scent and color into memory.

Cold winds pushed me into the lighted entry hall where my coworkers, Alma and Rosy, were already shaking off the chill.

"Ah, rain. No me le gusto, sí? I don't like esta noche."

Alma chattered "Spanglish," her concession to a common language, and Rosy ignored me with her usual benign indulgence. Even though we shared jokes, coffee and donuts, and complaints about hospital policies, Rosy closed herself off to me.

"Bad storm tonight." I fumbled for a pen and paper while Louise, the evening-shift nurse, paced around the small enclosure of desk, chart rack, and medicine cabinet.

"The first storms of the season are always the worst. November sets a chill in my bones that doesn't leave until May." She pulled on her rubber overshoes. "Come on, let's get report started so I can go home to a hot tub."

Before sitting down, I turned on the hall light and the second set of office lights. "It feels creepy in here tonight."

"This place can spook you until you get used to it," she laughed. "Wait until you've been around fourteen years, like me. Nothing about this place bothers me anymore."

I aspired to Louise's cool professionalism. She possessed the emotional distance that I believed distinguished the most competent nurses. She reported on the patients' conditions like a child reciting a poem. The rhythm pulled the matter-of-fact words along.

"Mr. Edwards' ulcer is worse today. Try to change his position every two hours tonight. Miss Wallace is going to the general hospital in the A.M. for a biopsy." She looked up as if to say *at last* but merely shook her head and continued her report. "Mary Cromer refused to eat again today. Maybe it's time for a feeding tube . . . or a psych consult. I left her doctor a note. John Kline . . . ," she broke the rhythm with a deep sigh. "John needed morphine twice on my time, twice on the day shift. He seems to be getting worse. The morphine barely holds him for four hours." She lit a cigarette. "Can you believe it, Janie? This is still a PRN order." Exhaling a cloud of smoke, she leaned toward me confidentially. "You know, I think his doctor is afraid John will get addicted if we give it around the clock. The poor guy probably doesn't have another month to go. I wish we could keep him comfortable." Crushing out the half-smoked cigarette, she stood abruptly. "Everyone else on the floor is stable. Come on, let's make rounds so I can get out of here."

I followed Louise in and out of the dim rooms as she made a final check at each bedside. I made notes of the bags, bottles, and tubes that were to occupy my hours. The rooms were populated with sleeping, groaning, babbling patients.

"Hey you, get me up! I've got to get . . . ouch, ouch."

"Now, now Betty, wherever do you have to get to at this hour?" Louise teased the shrunken, wrinkled lady in bed.

"Get away, girl," the old woman spit. "My leg hurts, my leg."

Louise and I freed Betty from the tangle of sheets. We moved pillows behind her back and between her knees, arranging her in a more comfortable position.

"There, isn't that better now, dear?" Louise cooed. As we left the room Louise told me, "Betty's getting crazier by the day. She's totally out of it. She talks all day to her dead husband, doesn't even recognize her son when he visits. I guess she keeps the day shift entertained." She shrugged. "Anyway, I hope you have a quiet night. I'm free at last."

Gray light, like evening fog, settled in the hospital corridors. Only the absence of darkness lightened the hallways. The rowdy storm outside rattled the window but did not disturb the palpable rhythm of the midnight quiet. It felt as though everyone was inhaling at the same time and slowly exhaling together.

At one A.M. rounds everyone was stable. Mr. Edwards had been turned on his side. Alma and Rosy cleaned up soiled patients, changed linens, added a needed blanket, and restrained a restless sleeper. I liked the pace of the night shift as it moved through its hours with the steady ticking of a clock. My only concern was that someone would die. No one had ever died on my shift. I felt a combination of shame and eagerness as I stood over a faltering patient, hoping he or she would live until eight A.M. Death scared me. I had no experience with it and thought of it as something ugly, painful, and vaguely contagious.

"Help me, help me please," a small voice cried.

"There go Betty otra vez. I change her sheets, but it no calm her. She unhappy vieja." Alma snapped her gum.

I did not know what more I could offer. She had already been given her tranquilizer for the night. "Maybe I'll sit with her awhile," I said to Rosy. She nodded.

"Oh dear, I'm so afraid." Betty's voice shook.

"It's OK, you're safe," I reassured her, stroking her large gnarled hands. Long ago they must have been useful and perhaps lovely, but now the nails were yellowed and splintered. I wondered about the crooked tip of her index finger. It looked as if it had been broken and never set right.

"They've all left me. I'm all alone," she cried. "Oh Charles. He never would let them do this to me. He never let me be alone so." The depth of her sigh caused a wheeze.

"What was Charles like?" I asked, knowing that by talking about him she might find solace.

"He was a good man. You know, a *real* man." Her thin voice pretended strength. "So handsome. All the other girls were jealous." Her eyes twinkled. "Yes, everyone looked up to him."

Before leaving the room I stroked her soft white hair. She had fallen back to what I hoped was a pleasant dream.

Wind and rain tapped a lullaby on the window panes. Three A.M. was always a difficult hour for me to keep my eyes open. I walked through the rooms, stopping at each bedside, wondering what the patients' lives had been before illness and age had wasted them. I made sure the bedrails were up and that everyone was breathing.

John Kline was awake.

"The pain's comin' in waves." A shadow of playfulness lingered about his mouth. "I'm waitin' ta see what crests with the next wave."

He stopped talking, eyes closed and lips taut. My fingertips resting on his wrist felt his pulse increase with the pain.

"No ship in sight. Send for the Marines. Suppose I could have my medicine now?"

It had been the required four hours since his last shot. "The Marines have landed," I whispered as I administered the morphine. Tomorrow the nurses could do battle with the doctor for more ammunition against John's pain.

A bedrail rattled in the next room. I found Betty half turned around in bed, mumbling to herself.

"Get me out of here! I want to see my Charles." A trace of anger flickered. "He'd get me out of here!" her gray eyes misted. "I don't know what happened." She slid back into confusion. "Joey used to be a good boy, but then Charles died and, I don't know. . . ." Her uncomprehending eyes looked to me. "Dear, do I know you? What's your name?"

"Janie. My name is Janie and I'm your nurse."

"My nurse?" She was indignant in an instant. "I don't need a nurse. I've always been the healthiest of all my sisters — Sadie, she's the sick one. What do I need a nurse for?"

"Betty, it's hard for you to walk, and your family wants you to be safe and cared for."

"I don't need to be taken care of," she snapped. "Joey's always helped me. It's only right. I looked after my mother 'til the day she died." Betty turned her face away from me. "It's not right, it's just not right." She lifted her big hands to reveal their emptiness. "But I can tell you one thing." Her steely eyes turned to me. "If Charles were here, things would be different. He'd tell you and your people to go to hell."

Pride slipped into weariness. Paper-thin eyelids closed. Her wheezing filled the room.

"Please, don't go yet." She placed her knobby hand over mine. "Oh mama," her tiny voice cracked.

The building shivered in the cold wind. I heard Rosy exclaim, "Lord, what a night!" from down the hall. Icy rain slamming into the sill startled Betty.

"Quick, answer the door. I wonder who that could be?"

"It's only the weather, that's all. A storm," I whispered.

"A storm? I didn't know. I must watch for Charles. My glasses. I can't see. Where are my glasses?"

I placed very smudged bifocals on her shrunken face. In the dim hospital light she looked like an owl — eyes wide open looking into the night.

"Now dear, help me to the window. I've got to get to the window. Charles will be home soon." She pulled up her knees to swing herself out of bed. Her ankle fell between the bars of the siderail.

I untied the knot she had made with her legs, the siderail, and the linens, and helped her to sit on the edge of the bed, the flat of my hand supporting her bent back. She felt like nothing more than a bundle of twigs.

"Let's sit here a moment and rest."

"I've rested enough," she growled, her heavy hand pressed into my knee for leverage as she stood. It was a slow shuffle to the window. I tried to surround her thin body with my arms, my feet close to her leaden steps as she dragged across the linoleum floor, filling the room with her whistle and wheeze. Fixing her magnified gray eyes on a point on the window, she drew nearer as if guided by an invisible pulley. Goosebumps crawled over my skin and my palms were sweating, but I held her up as we proceeded. I craned my neck back toward the door, hoping that Rosy or Alma would appear. I never should have let this happen, but Betty's insistence was stronger than my fear.

Her long crooked fingers clung to the windowsill like a bird to a branch. I supported her waist while she leaned forward to peer out.

"I can see him coming up the road." Her frail body tensed with excitement.

I looked out the window. It was a dark night; the branches blowing against the pane were barely visible.

Betty stared hard into the night. "Oh, he works so hard, that old guy," she whispered. Her voice lightened into a song, almost a laugh. "Quick, Joey, can you smell the wisteria? It's so sweet."

Then she sank, quickly, painlessly into my arms. I nearly dropped her I was so surprised. In the breath of the second that precedes a thought, I understood — death had relieved her. The complete stillness when her wheezing ceased scared me. I struggled to carry her now-heavy body to the bed.

Deafened by the pounding of my own heart, I ran to find Alma and Rosy.

"I shouldn't have let her out of bed! I knew it!" Tears showed my confusion. "This never happened to me before." I searched their faces for a suggestion of what to do.

"Janie, calm yourself." Alma wrapped her long arm around my shoulders. "She was una vieja." She shrugged. "She died, rest her soul in heaven. We will finish the colecciones and IV for you while you take care of business." When she kissed my cheek I smelled her flowery perfume that had not faded during the night.

"You know," I said to Rosy, whose eyes revealed compassion, "she said she saw her husband. That was all she seemed to want really. I'm sort of glad, if she saw him like that, you know, at the end."

Rosy's smile offered me a moment of comfort.

"I don't know, I don't know." I paced in a tight circle. "Am I responsible?"

"No, Janie, you didn't do nothing. The old lady died because it was God's will, not yours. That mean old lady is in everlasting peace right now. She's not a joke for nobody."

Rosy's words helped to calm me into reason. The necessary phone calls were made, the paperwork completed.

As dawn ignited the dark sky, the sounds of early risers could be heard. Old machines cranking their engines, doubtful people looking to see if they were still alive, and groaning as they realized they had awakened into their nightmare. I opened the window in Betty's room. The storm was ending. Wet earth perfumed the cold air. Winter was coming, but for a moment I could almost smell the wisteria.

Instructing a New Mother

DAWN RAMM *Fairfield, California*

Like a Little Barracuda
   the newborn latches on—
      nurses until a nipple bleeds.
Move him to the other breast,
   I advise—
speak for the hospital
and for the numerous books
I have read:
     how to hold him
     how to open his mouth
     how to break the suction
            with a finger.
Yet I never knew my body
     as this mother does—
       its natural capacity.
I measured exact amounts
of evaporated milk,
      Karo syrup and water.
The efficient nurse who contaminated
           nothing.

The Demonstration

DAWN RAMM *Fairfield, California*

Threads of blood arc
as I peel away the bandage
from the tumor on his neck
        He cannot speak.

He writes furious notes —
how yesterday
I spread the lotion
so thick it melted
all day in sticky rivulets.

His lover takes the jar.
Tenderly she lays the salve —
a glittering film
across the gray crevices.

Over and over her arms
circle him in an embrace
of trailing gauze that buries
the strangling mass.
A hump she tapes and strokes
as if it were their child
        she dressed.

How will I chart?
That she needs more instruction?
That she forgot her gloves?
That it doesn't matter?

Mr. Craig and His Wife

DAWN RAMM *Fairfield, California*

Apology to the dying woman
for thinking her husband her son —
my lap balancing paperwork —
my pen aimed at the space
for responsible person.
I cross out son, write husband.

Never opening her eyes
she had corrected me.
Her head deep in the pillow —
her body barely a fold
            under the blanket.

I teach him terminal care
so that he knows her
more intimately
than she had ever allowed.
They joke about that.

My visits are only a statement
            of availability.
Even when her heart fluttered
into its final rhythm —
it was his fingers on her pulse,

his arms holding her until heat
left her. Until she stiffened —
until her death was confirmed
by uncomfortable strangers.

Where Are You Now, Ella Wade?

JOYCE RENWICK *Iowa City, Iowa*

We climb the tower of the Ravner Building and find Miss Bendix at the desk. She's gray and thin as grass. No cap. No crisp uniform as we remember. She wears a lab coat over street clothes and on her name pin, a long meaningless title.

She smiles. "Today you have our Ella." Miss Bendix is still head nurse.

Ella's in the corner bed. Our nerves jangled, we find comfort in the Zen-like sameness of her care. We escape to her as threatened children might escape to a bedroom corner with the dolls, or up a backyard tree.

Ella has been comatose for years. The early portions of her chart are off the floor in the caverns of Medical Records or maybe lost. We do not know her age.

"Ella." We call her name to humanize her body. "Ella. Ella Wade."

Her eyes are open, unblinking.

In surgery, while she sat upright in a chair, they hinged a bony trapdoor in her skull, and someone peered inside to hear the hollow echoes of her mind. Then they closed the door. Her head was shaved before the craniotomy. Somehow her hair follicles were persuaded to shut down as well. She remains forever bald. She's our dusky Nefertiti, her bare head wrapped in cotton. Dark lashes kohl her eyes. Her egg-shaped head is covered by stockinet, a hat made from a sleeve of clinging cotton. It's gathered at the crown with rubber bands, and at her forehead rolled, a ski-cap diadem.

"Hello, Ella." We stroke her hand. "How are you?" In her silence, she is an infant without cry, without want, without future. "Can you hear us, Ella?"

We turn our Nefertiti in the bulrushes of her bed. On the rivulets of her sheets she is like a log bobbing in our minds. Outside the hospital window, birds cling to the trees like fruit.

"Ella," we call her. "Ella." She is a mirror in which our fantasies play. In the air of our imaginations we hear a whispered response.

If we left Ella in the tower in a lonely room, would she awaken, sit up in bed, and wonder? Or is there still upon her lips the poison taste of bitter almond, or sweetness crystallized to coma long ago? Did a tumor eat her mind? An auto shock her with such impact she didn't want to know?

Her easy breathing says she's lost in there. She does not fight our good intentions. Her body is neither stiff nor heavy. One person can position her. Without the weight of consciousness — as innocent as dawn before the wires fused forever left with right — she's light. So light we think sometimes she seeps from her trapdoor into the air above us. She has a fondness for us, we imagine, as baby loves the breast or as a lover, for a moment, loves the loved.

We stand by her bed and watch the intern dig a house key up the soles of her feet. The response to the Babinski test says, no malingering. She's really gone. We are wordless wind in the bare room of her mind. We do not ask each other what private dream sustains us in her care.

"She's blind," the intern says. But we think no. We insist that Ella sees us. She records her view on film, in a golden box in her head she'll one day open. The intern strides away.

Ella must do nothing but keep intact her flawless skin. Stroked, bathed, lubricated around the clock by generations of nurses, protected from sun and padded against injury, her skin's integrity is unbroken.

She breathes without assistance. No supplemental oxygen, no airway, her ribs retract, flesh out, retract, flesh out, like bony gills. Her lips are buds of flesh above a toothless mouth. Her teeth have been removed for "ease of care," and yet in our minds we return them: broad, strong, slightly yellow. Why, we ask, no dignity of teeth?

We help her modest swimming in her Nile of air. We take her through her strokes — crawl and back and breast. We exercise her long thin arms, slim legs. We bathe her. We call her name again, again, massaging her buttocks and along her spine. We feed her through a tube coiled at her belly.

"Ella," we say. "Ella Wade. How does it feel to have a belly full?"

We move Ella's limbs in the directions they should go. We circle around the clock-face of Ella's body; the range-of-motion exercises are as orderly as a clock tower that works. First the right arm at nine o'clock, left arm at three. Left leg at five o'clock, the right at seven. We flex her wrists, her elbows, her knees. We circle her extremities, like chopsticks in dry bowls, in the sockets of her shoulders and her hips.

We name the bones as mantra as we go: humerus—radius—ulna—carpals—metacarpals—phalanges, then femur—tibia—fibula—tarsals—metatarsals, phalanges again. Again, and more. Sometimes we speak of nursery rhymes or saints. Sometimes we name the angels that we know: Gabriel, Michael, Aziel, Raziel, Arios. We spread her fingers wide and lift each phalange toward the ceiling, to stretch against the always stronger muscles of contraction. We know this uneven muscle strength, this natural move toward closure, keeps us neat. Like a door upon a spring, the loose limbs stow themselves along the body.

Miss Bendix comes around and helps us flip Ella on her side, more a gesture of bonhomie, we know, than a response to some real need. We wonder if Miss Bendix still has the heart to sing.

"Is Ella as you remember her?" she asks. She smiles.

"Yes, Miss Bendix. Quite the same."

"We change." Miss Bendix flits a finger through her graying hair. "But Ella stays the same."

Miss Bendix turns, is gone.

We place a pillow between our Ella's knees to keep them free of chafing, to air our Ella's private parts, to keep her sweet. We've put a footboard on the bed, a wooden earth beneath her for when she's stretched full length. And when she's turned every other hour for sprinting in the air, sandbags keep her feet from curling. Her easy breathing says she's lost in there.

Those feet are slim and arched, the ankles thin. Her toes overlap upon each other. Her first toes ride upon her great toes. Her smallest toes seek their sisters to claim less space upon the earth, we guess. But still, we keep her foot soles flat against a surface, careful that her toes don't drop, or she'll be hobbling to eternity on pointe—or three-inch heels—the ball joints of her hips and shoulders frozen too.

Left alone, a body curls into itself like cold-shocked leaves. We who stretch Ella to extension six times a day have kept her flexible enough to dream without deformity. But still, we know our efforts will not heal her.

Her mouth opens and we wait. There is no sound. In a moment, her eyes squint into a yawn.

We listen for the voice that never comes, an ancient chant perhaps, a song. We know after a stroke, the smash-up of a cerebral vascular accident, those mute to spoken words can often sing—a different portion of the brain engages song—and in our mind's ear we hear our Ella singing scat, or Billie Holiday, or Billy Swan, or rap.

Her hands rest at her sides now, where we've placed them. She can do anything with these hands in our imaginations. We see her grip the throttle of a plane, towing training targets above the trees. Steady, steady. Finished, she pulls the plane into a climb. She climbs, climbs more, and then the twisting curl away of her chandelle.

Her fingers are square-ended, the moons distinct, pale yellow on the oblong nails. We tuck into her palms the taped white washcloth rolls we make for her. She holds them loosely like batons for a relay race she never runs. We make them to protect her from the moist dark of her own hands. The nails of her contracted fingers would pierce her palms. We marvel how her nails grow and get dirty. Ella digs potatoes in her dreams.

Our lives make noise, we know, and wounds. We scan her body to look for proof of her participation, and find not scar, but evidence. On her long body for the first time we focus on a faint dark line from umbilicus to mons. How could we have missed it, the unfaded *linea negra* of a pregnancy. She is not pregnant now. What's left is just a shadow. Oh, we say, our mouths circular wounds upon our faces. She ran eclamptic into coma with a child. And now she's caught in a refusal, forever stuck in the body that will slow, slow, and one day stop.

If we peer out of the corners of our eyes, a subtle light still comes from Ella's body, a pale light most people take note of only when it's gone. What is there in us, we ask, that keeps believing our Ella will someday emerge into the world, like a small fox, its eyes newly opened, clawing out of its burrow. How startling will be the sun that day, how blue the sky. We know we keep believing this because we must.

She yawns, our Nefertiti. We think she needs some space, some air.

"Ella," we ask whispering, "would you wake if we no longer needed you?"

We see her, bewigged and dentured, standing on a street corner at a bus stop. Her brown doll eyes are lined in black. She's squinting in the sun. She clutches fare coins tightly to her chest and sings out to us.

"My bus is coming." She waves. "Here it is."

Back Rub

DEBRA J. SANDY *Madison, Wisconsin*

Mrs. Joseph died today
We were diagnosed the same week
almost
the same day . . .

Her cancer was in her bones already
They told me my disease is under control
I'm going home tomorrow
What time is it?
3 A.M.?
I'm afraid.

There's a bake sale at my granddaughter's school next week
She's seven
My daughter has never mastered *my* brownies.

John brought Mrs. Joseph roses last week
He tells me our lawn has suffered
it's been so dry
We were married in college
He hates to mow the lawn.

Do you have children?
Your hands are so warm . . .
Mrs. Joseph had six children
Have you always worked nights?
Isn't it lonely?

John's picking me up at ten
He brought me roses today
Yesterday
only 3 A.M.?
we celebrated the news

We'll have a nice celebration at home
we'll have pot roast.

I always add cinnamon and allspice to my pot roast
It's my secret
John won't eat pot roast except at home
it's his favorite.

I always have fresh clothes brought in to wear home
I don't like wearing the same thing as when I come in
it's a habit I've gotten into
My clothes fit differently now.

Maybe I should buy some new clothes
to celebrate — the New Me —
Mrs. Joseph's hair came back so curly
It had been straight
Mine's still straight
You have my hair style.

My daughter's pregnant again
She's due in June
I was diagnosed in June
It will be one year when the baby is born
I'll be there — I'm lucky
I'm afraid.

Sounds at Night: 1960

ADELE GERMAINE SARRAZIN *Montebello, California*

The chimes of the chapel clock striking one.
The chirping of treetoads.
The echoing roar of a truck going down the freeway
rising to a crescendo and then fading into the distance.
The monotonous whirring of the refrigerator motor.
The symphony of hungry babies.
The slamming of a car door heralding the advent
of another mother-to-be.
The repeated jangle of the doorbell revealing
taut nerves or — need of speed.
The shrill cry of a laboring woman.
The ticking of a clock.
A siren's wail of need for room to pass.
The ringing phone and a worried father's inquiry
about his screaming baby's first night home.
The tinkle of glass and the gurgle of water being poured.
The squeak of bedsprings, and the shuffle of slippers —
a mother on the way to the bathroom.
The keys clinking together while opening the locked cupboard
for the pain-relieving drugs.
The grunt of a labor soon to be terminated.
Bells awakening the sisters for meditation.
The smooth, rubber-tired swish of the cart going to the delivery
    room.
Footsteps hurrying down the corridor — *Doctor, the patient is
    ready.*
The doctor giving orders in a monotone.
The nurses, soothing, saying, *Breathe deeply.*
A newborn's cry.
The excited query of the new father and grandmother,
How much does he weigh?
The audible, even breathing of a new mother in exhausted sleep.
The swish of a mop in its chore of preparing the delivery room
for another patient.

The clatter of instruments being cleaned.
The peculiar plop of gloves being turned.
The bell of the nearby church, summoning worshippers
to early Mass.

Who Owns the Libretto?

JUDY SCHAEFER *Harrisburg, Pennsylvania*

They browsed quickly through
The medical stacks
Text after text
Pushing page after page
He watched her quick movements
He held her gray coat
To allow her armroom
And give her space to breathe
She pulled from
Shelf after shelf
Bent on her knees
Stretched up her arms
Then leaned back and sat down
Lifted her knees as in
Stirrup for childbirth
Book after hardbound book
Looking for a gush of water
Found one
This one
Splash of a waterfall
Look at this one
Pointed him to it
The illness there
Their respirations now fast
The illness of their child
Described with paragraphical details
Graphs and diagrams
Percentages and prognoses
They looked
Side to side
Held their breath
So as not to be caught
In their act
Not to be scolded

In their act of love
Their moment of near death
The inner sanctum
Stacks on stacks
Of well-worded knowledge
Of medical texts
An act of suspicion
That would confirm
    or deny
What the doctors told

Medicine from the Wood

JUDY SCHAEFER *Harrisburg, Pennsylvania*

Wooed by juniper berries
And promises of bitter persimmon buds
We remain long in this wood
I carry all the proofs
To your bedside
Like a radiologist
Whose specialty is artifact
In a tightly woven basket
Gray slate with fossil fern
Soft mounds of moss
    still earth warm
Fish tails in stone from Galway Bay
Pine cones
Pine resin
Hickory nuts
Hikers' orange peel
And silvery spider web
And the kiss of a mayfly

Long Hospital Stay

JUDY SCHAEFER *Harrisburg, Pennsylvania*

From the end of the corridor
A four year old looked at the tunnel
Of movement, trays and carts
Gondola meetings
Through guarded eyes
Through a venetian blind
   squeaky water clean
   white soft-soled shoes
   drawers and doors
   and needle caps
   rings, beepers and bleeps
He pulled them open and closed
Adjusted them to keep out
The flow of alcohol and betadine
Or to let it in, sliver by sliver
He just watched
Watched for snags of limb and branch
Shadows of wolf and bear
Tiny sentinel who moved
An invisible cord of golden twine
That called upon flute and chime
We would forget what he had
Seen and heard
We would forget
That he was a child
And he would fall asleep finally
On a rickety river raft
With hand still pulling
To protect his dreams

Sunday Morning

JUDY SCHAEFER *Harrisburg, Pennsylvania*

From the hospital's fifth floor
across the street, the cars
breeze from the red brick
church's parking lot as if from
a car wash, fast and now clean
I have prayed in those stalls
I have gone on my knees in those stalls
A showboat, slow and unmoving
sits high on the ice-logged river
its currents deep with sluggish
catfish and sandy silt
I have danced on that barge
I have flirted and caroused on that barge
I applaud the tourists' view
of the Missouri, of the red
French riverbank church
the parade of small St. Charles homes
with peaked heavenward
roofs and square yards
waiting for crocus and tulip
I am grateful to the church
red solid and watchful of me
I hear the ghosts of fur
traders and French priests
and the rub of wagons going west
across unpaved parking lots, I feel
the deceitful river shift and rise
in my middle-aged breast
I await the doctor coming from
the complacencies of the peignoir
and late coffee with my father's
diagnosis, I applaud
as if I need a doctor to tell me
that his wit is gone

The nurses watch my nurse's watching
Tsk tsk to me of Sunday morning
I would have paid for this view
on any other Sunday, I applaud
the view of my new generation
and watch the gathering of another
congregation, for the second Mass on the riverbank,
to praise a slippery slow-
moving God, I look up to see
the priest come in the back room
with a wave to the early faithful
comfortable in their pew place
And the river mocks me
with its icy refusal to move
Then the church bells boom
out, arrogant and noisy
Vibrations ripple to the showboat
the fifth floor and every little
house, and the crocused ground
The river moves not a crystal
not a knife sliver of its burden
Quiet descends
Now a surprise
A silent flock
I felt
the flutter
pass by
Geese fly in V overhead
moving smoothly behind the steeple
Their rhythmic soft wing, the most
encouraging thing I have seen
this Sunday morning; I fly with them
and give up my heart to their sky

Feather and Claw

JUDY SCHAEFER *Harrisburg, Pennsylvania*

Birds fly in and out
And take my soul
On their wing
Midnight nurses
With penlight bones
Hollowed flutes
I hear the rattle
of their coming
And their going
I feel their beaks
Sharp tongues
Feeding on me
They take piece
By small piece
In the hours
Before the sun
I am amused
With wonder
At this leave-
Taking of me
Escher fins and fishes
Of air and sea
I beg aphasic
To leave something

Rehab Nursing

JUDY SCHAEFER *Harrisburg, Pennsylvania*

This is where my heart is, over here
in the niches and the small worry knots
in the crack and crevice of curbstone
of slanted path and walkway
A step that begins with a wiggle
of a toe, recall of a cindered road
chips and scattered stone
See how the tiny mosses grow
so slow
Observance through the night
is an unrewarding chore
See how the tiny mosses grow
sprigs unseen
roots tenacious
quiet tender shoots
bandaged still
until one bright sunsplashed moment
on the rock
above the salty pulsing surf
This is made of climate, rain and sun
storm and lightning
and washed out bridges
and new canals
This is where I am, over here
in the cinder path with you

Black Stockings and Me

ELSIE SCHMIED *Oak Ridge, Tennessee*

There weren't many things I hated in this world as much as I hated black stockings. And yet I tolerated them for three long years when I was a student nurse in Milwaukee. Our student uniform was as attractive as a shroud. Shapeless, sand-colored, white-collared, short-sleeved, and belted, the dress sagged half-way between my knees and ankles when other eighteen year olds wore knee-length skirts. The two lumpy patch pockets always bulged with pens, scissors, and notepads. We even had to wear cotton undergarments to prevent sparking an explosion of anesthetic gases in the operating room. I tolerated cotton slips, but I detested black stockings. The black stockings and shoes we students were required to wear with the uniform were the final indignity.

Sister said we had to have black stockings before we went on the hospital floors in our sixth week. My folks and I searched the stores in our spare time, but black stockings were as rare as chocolate bars during the war. By the end of the fifth week, I still had none. In desperation, my mother dyed six pairs of tan cotton hose black. I was ready.

My first patient contact: evening care for three patients. This meant helping them with their toileting needs, washing their hands and faces, and brushing their teeth. We, who had never touched a stranger, had to wash backs and give back rubs with rubbing alcohol and talcum powder. Even worse, everyone knew we were only "probationers," with hairnets, not nurses' caps, on our heads. I tried to do my assignments perfectly, but other patients turned their signal lights on and doctors stopped me in the halls, asking questions. I was so nervous, my hands were wet with perspiration; my first three hours on duty were like three years.

Somehow, all my patients ate their suppers and I finished their care. The head nurse inspected the ward, found dust on the base of one overbed table, said I was adequate, and dismissed me for the evening. I hurried back to the nurses' home.

Safe in my room, I kicked my black shoes off. The linings were damp. I peeled my garter belt and stockings off. My feet were black as coal! I tried to scrub the color off without luck; five minutes before study hall, I dried my gray feet, threw on some clothes, ankle socks and saddle shoes, and dashed downstairs.

For two months my feet ranged in color from dead black to ash gray. The black dye stayed on the body of the hose, but the color from the feet of the stockings transferred to my feet and to the lining of the shoes until everything was a dirty gunmetal color.

By December, things had settled down, but the life of a student nurse in the mid-forties was far from glamorous. The meals were mostly starch, and there was never enough food to satisfy the appetite of a growing girl; I hid jars of peanut butter in my dresser and ate it by the spoonful. It was routine to work eight hours, go to class for three or four more, and then study. On my two half-days off I slept or studied, living in constant fear that I'd never learn enough to be a good nurse.

But I was becoming more skillful with patients, practicing first on our mannequin, Mrs. Chase, and my feet slowly faded. Best of all, my father scoured the city during his lunch hours until he found some black rayon stockings in a hosiery store downtown and gave me three pairs as a Christmas gift. How I treasured them; *they* didn't dye my feet.

During our second year, we met students from other hospitals, most of whom were also plagued with black stockings, except for those from a fancy Eastside hospital; they wore white shoes and stockings. Our class agreed that our uniform would be far more attractive without black shoes and stockings, and we petitioned the director of nursing. She refused to listen. Tradition, she said. Counting down our 1,095 student days and looking forward to graduation, we dreamed of white stockings and fashionably short skirts.

One evening, a visitor handed me a package and thanked me for caring for his wife during her pneumonia crisis. He gave a similar package to every student on the unit, and the head nurse said we could keep them. Inside the box were three pairs of the first nylon stockings I had ever seen—sheer as cobwebs and seamed up the back. Our grateful visitor owned a hosiery store.

I wore my precious black nylons every Sunday until graduation. Meanwhile, our class bought fitted, short-skirted uniforms and the much desired white stockings and shoes, long before the big day. On August 28, 1947, our class of twenty-one paraded proudly in crisp, fitted white uniforms, white stockings and shoes, and starched white caps to receive our school pins on graduation day.

The following month, a young Frenchman named Christian Dior showed his first collection, "The New Look," featuring longer skirts, about halfway between the knee and ankle. His models pranced down the runway wearing sheer black stockings with their pumps.

Sometimes you just can't win.

Rhythms

BETHANY SCHROEDER *Sunnyvale, California*

Karl says we flatter ourselves
in trying to save a life. He hates
the confusion of hands on unfamiliar flesh,
the clatter of stainless steel and plastic
pushed to an excess of excellence.
He hates the blood on his smock
got there by our vain resistance
to some stranger's death.
He wants the green walls to be quiet,
the mayo stands lined up
beside empty beds, the surgical lights
kept off in response to a vision
that lets life proceed how it will.
He wants the careful truck
of cell to cell to state such harmonies
as angels know.

              When he puts
his hands on men
who can no longer put
their hands on him, he says he hates
our overrated reliance on skill.
We should dismiss the grief
in love grown too completely physical
when hearts refuse their difficult rhythms
and lungs will not fill,
will not consent to a relationship
with air. He calls our care
indulgence and thinks we'd do better
to make less noise about the life
we will not let go gracefully back to God.

Morning Visitors

ELLEN SHAY *Palo Alto, California*

Mr. Johnson doesn't look so good today. I noticed it as soon as I walked into the room this morning. As I go through his chart, all the numbers are the same. His vital signs and his labs are all rock stable. He's been here a long time, not looking very good, but today he looks a little greener or bluer or whiter, or something. Perhaps the smell in the room has changed, or the ventilator sounds a little more high-pitched. I can't put my finger on what it is, but something is different. . . . His immobile features give me no clues for what's giving me this sense of deterioration.

Even in a coma he seems to be maintaining a dignified expression. I imagine him saying to me, "Don't worry, dear, I'm fine," but I feel uneasy as I go about his familiar morning care and medications. He looks like such a nice man, and he would no doubt be mortified by the spectacle of his stuffing coming out, as he leaks onto the bed like a sawdust doll.

Mrs. Johnson, the wife, is very gracious and soft-spoken. Her clothes are elegant and her hair is always beauty-parlor perfect. Her face is wrinkled but still beautiful, and her eyes are clear blue. She comes in every day and asks the same questions. Things don't change much. She stands quietly by his bed, always refusing to sit down, and squeezes his hand.

I recognize the even sound of her heels before she enters the room. I've fixed him up to look nice for her visit, but he still looks below par. She enters, scans the room, and then looks as though she smells smoke. We discuss his lungs, his vital signs, the plan of the day, all the usual things. There is no concrete change to offer her, as we look at each other's worried faces.

"I don't know why, but he doesn't look as good today," I finally say.

"No, he doesn't. He looks sadder today," she says positively.

She goes to take her place by the bed, and I take my cue to leave the room for awhile. She always leaves at the same time, before the next round of medications and treatments. She wouldn't dream of being a bother.

I imagine the two of them going out for dinner, probably to a nice place where they know the owners and order the same dishes each time. They eat slowly, drink slowly, talk quietly, enjoy each other's company. . . . He squeezes her hand under the table.

* * *

The consciousness in Mr. Johnson's brain is like an eel languidly S-ing through smooth dark weeds. A few rays of light from the water's surface make little spotlights on the sea bottom, but mostly the eel S-es along in dull monotonous ecstasy.

A cluster of neurons in the frontal lobe simultaneously galvanize themselves for the struggle to be Mr. Johnson. "I am not an eel!" they cry. Mr. Johnson floats to the surface. One lidless eye just manages to break the surface tension of the water and take in the upper world. A spaghetti of plastic tubing threaded through a bank of blinking pumps is above his head, and the tubing snakes toward his head and chest. His chest is being mechanically inflated with bigger whooshes of air than feels comfortable.

Mr. Johnson gasps like a fish beached on a merry-go-round. The ventilator shrieks in outrage at having its cycle thrown out of phase. His vital signs climb upward on the monitor until the alarms are all going off.

Mr. Johnson's bedside is usually a harmonious humming of happy machines, but right now all the alarms are going off. I scurry over to see what's going on and I'm happy to see that his vital signs have gone up instead of down. I walk closer to his bed and see one eye is just barely open and darting around like a sardine. His body tenses up and one arm stirs, just a little. The hand on the awakened arm starts groping around.

I take and squeeze his hand, partly to keep it from grabbing any of his equipment, and speak directly into his good ear.

"Mr. Johnson, you're in the intensive care unit." His eye darts toward me and stays, but looks unfocused.

"You've been here about a month. Your heart is healing. You're doing okay. Your wife comes in every day to be with you. She just left."

These are the most encouraging things I can say without lying.

"Mr. Johnson, can you squeeze my hand?"

He squeezes my hand spasmodically, and then he suddenly looks gray and exhausted. His hand and arm go limp, his eye closes, and his vital signs sink back down to their usual numbers.

Mr. Eel Johnson sinks back to the seabottom. He thrashes around a moment and then goes back to S-ing through the smooth dark weeds.

Another Night, Another Customer

ELLEN SHAY *Palo Alto, California*

Mr. Omni is lying on his back, as inert as possible without actually being dead. Bored, I glance at him occasionally from my muscle magazine. I can't see his head over his mountainous belly.

At my next glance, his bed is empty. I'm looking around and starting to feel flustered, when I spot him. He's taped face up to the ceiling with long strips of bandage tape. It looks to me like he could remain there safely for a long time. I go back to my muscle magazine. Triceps, biceps, rectus femoris. . . .

Hours pass and treatments and medications are due, so I push a bed under him. He falls into it, nicely positioned and as bland as ever. I give him many different substances, pushing them into many different tubes. The proper sequence is important, and timing takes a certain knack. The colors must be right, as well as the amount of pressure generated. If things aren't just right, the customer turns into a rubber fish or a rutabaga.

I then unpack and repack several large holes in his thorax with expensive fibrous materials and adjust the angles of his limbs. I try to make him look like a real person by combing his hair and setting his chin at a proud angle. Then I go back to my muscle magazine.

Vietnam Canon

DANA SHUSTER *Chicago, Illinois*

Counting pulses and marking measures, she notes
clamorous tempos staccato and terrified,
sprightly meters syncopated and shocky,
sinuous adagios and ultimate arpeggios
sliding down codas of boogie-woogie boylives.

Amid bebop, bluegrass, hardrock warriors
she feels one small boysoul conducting Mozart
Eine Kleine Nachtmusik on the border of Cambodia,
his countenance evocative of El Greco
his age more apropos of Beatles
But men and wars do have a way
    of mixing things up.

Curandera

DANA SHUSTER *Chicago, Illinois*

A magnet seeking iron, my soul sought her source
in ancient mystical feminine sancta.
I dreamed of back alleys in Samarkand,
medieval murmurs in cold, damp cloisters —
vapored knowledge of birth, life, death,
throbbing mystery and sultry ritual,
fables passed furtively, one lifegiver to another
witcheries treasured since the debut of time.

Memorizing anatomy my brain envied answers;
chemistry, pharmacology lured my lust.
Shadowing the nuns I coveted the magic;
lurking in libraries I sniffed for secrets;
I practiced on oranges the tricks of the trade.
Awaiting anointment in the capping ceremony,
checking the mirror for a glimpse of the aura,
craving the quiver of sorceress flesh,
in the dark of my closet I willed my fingers
to glow with the power
the touch of the forbidden
the trace of the divine
the talent for miracles
the power to heal.

A year later beneath my secular hands
lies Humpty-Dumpty in green fatigues.
Forsaken by grace in an unholy place
this boy and I run out of time.
He will never grow withered and old,
I am a crone forever after this day.
I do nothing save hold his hand
until someone he trusts
beckons from the other side.

As my reflection dims in his eyes
he whispers a thank you;
his deathsmile grants me the goal of my quest.
At that sacred moment I know
I know
I am the healer.
The magic is mine.

NICU

DANA SHUSTER *Chicago, Illinois*

Dying babies need
    warmth
        motion
           song.

Dead babies need
           nothing.

Why am I still
        rocking
        singing?

Rochester, Minnesota, 1965

KELLY SIEVERS *Portland, Oregon*

Hot tunnels wound beneath the ground,
hospital to dormitory to chapel. But we

chose to run through icy
air. With stiff white wings pinned

to our heads, we hugged our breasts
and flew. From women draped

in long folds of white we learned
to pull back blankets, expose one

arm, one leg, to bathe
the sick. *Here is the heart,*

Sister Ruth said, showing us the empty
chambers, valves held tight

on tiny strings. *And the eye,*
one big black cow's eye,

its crystalline vitreous
hidden. Beneath the light from

three-story windows we sat on gallery
benches to watch silent men

open the brain. At night
we dipped our fingers

in holy water then slid
into our single beds,

hiding our hot
and steaming hearts.

Between the Heartbeats

KELLY SIEVERS *Portland, Oregon*

Will I dream? she asks, before I push
the syringe of drugs. She tells me of her dream
the night before: the doctor was pulling
yarn from her abdomen. Red, yellow, green
it flowed down the table, across the floor,
filling the room. In one corner sat her son
coiling skeins; in another, her daughter
knitting. She sleeps now. For stories spun
between each heartbeat, I listen.
Who has loved her? What home holds her?
She weaves her dreams in silence.
The life I see, I measure
in minutes, keeping watch
over its tangled knot.

Before Heart Surgery

KELLY SIEVERS *Portland, Oregon*

Day after day I watch them enter the body
through the soft flesh of the belly. Knife burning
fat, hands running the bowel searching
for kinks, or cancer, they operate.

But the heart is a different matter, reserved
for special teams. Too close to the soul, I decided
long ago. "Where is the soul?" I would ask. "Here,"
Sister Rose would say, folding her hands
over her heart.

I saw them open the chest once, dividing the firm bone
of the sternum with the round blade of a cast cutter:
the body thrown on the table, a bullet wound clean
beside a nipple, "*Let's crack his chest!*" And his heart
was empty. His pupils, wide and dark, told us
his soul had escaped.

"No, I don't *do* hearts anymore," I tell my friend the night
before his surgery, remembering rising before dawn, filling
row after row of syringes with drugs to relieve the heart's
pressures, strengthen its force, control
erratic beats.

"*We're going in, watch the heart,*" they would shout. "*Stand by*
to go on pump." *Blood whirled through coils. The heart*
stopped. And where was the soul? Dancing on the globes
of the lights? Held tight in the arms of a lover
who waited outside the door? Or did the soul hide,
deep in the belly?

Breath

KELLY SIEVERS *Portland, Oregon*

In the old days we taped a cotton ball
to the end of the nose, so we could watch
      the white ball flutter
each time breath left the body. We peered
through the window of a lead-shielded door,
      counting.

I am more comfortable closer, one hand
holding the patient's head, one finger feeling
      blood pulse
over the notch in his jawbone. My other
hand surrounds the breathing bag. I wait
      for each breath

to begin. I follow respiration's
rhythm, sense how much more air
      lungs need.
Breath moves softly against the chest
wall. I have learned how air moves easily through
      willing lungs.

Breathe deep, my yoga teacher shows me today.
      My belly swells.
Think only of the breath, and follow it. Breath fills
my chest, flows into my arms, my neck,
      down my spine,
I follow it, trying to feel
      closer
      to my life.

The Journey

ROSEMARY SMITH *Mid Glamorgan, Wales*

Escorting patients "to" and "from" hospital had always been a nursing duty I enjoyed. One such journey occurred on a cold winter's morning in December.

The ambulance was due at nine A.M., and I had prepared my patient for the journey ahead. Danny was six months old, a patient on the children's ward for three months; now he was being transferred to a children's home thirty miles away.

He was a handsome babe with curly jet-black hair, and his emerald eyes were almost magical. He had always been a hungry little thing, and on that particular morning, as soon as the teat of the bottle touched his lips, he opened his mouth wide, like a nestling, sucking hard until there was nothing left but air, his eyelids fluttering with pure delight.

After his usual morning bath, I dressed him in a new blue knit suit and packed his red suitcase with new clothes, knitted or donated by well-wishers. A brown cardboard box held his favorite toys, given to him by the nursing staff.

The ambulance was punctual, and, after a tearful farewell, we began our journey. Apart from the ambulance driver, Danny and I were the only passengers on that cold morning. I held him tightly in my arms and thought about the suffering he had endured at the hands of his parents, and how he had been condemned to a life of darkness.

We passed through a busy shopping center, and through the tinted windows of the ambulance I saw brightly colored lights and decorations strung in preparation for the Christmas festivities. People rushed in and out of stores, caught up in the madness of shopping. I wondered about Danny's future; what could the holidays mean to him? I recalled my daughter's delight at seeing a Christmas tree lit up, and how wide-eyed she had been the first time she had seen Father Christmas. Danny would never see any of these sights.

We came to a pelican crossing and allowed a young mother

pushing her pram with two children in tow to cross. She resembled a mother hen with her chicks on her tail. I thought of Danny's mother. Why did she abandon him?

During the journey I began to look at the natural features of the South Wales valleys. I had read poems that spoke of such beauty, but I wondered how I could possibly describe the picturesque scenery to someone like Danny, who had been blinded as a baby. How could I ever express the color of green, or define the rich yellows, browns, reds, or oranges that I saw as I looked out over the valley with its field of bare trees and fallen leaves? Perhaps I could have found words for the more desolate stretches of our journey, the blackened landscapes, flattened and uninteresting, only the remains left where a colliery once stood.

As we neared the children's home, I realized how quiet Danny had been, and how I longed for him to give me a smile, or even to cry out to let me know that he felt the same sadness that I felt. He opened his eyes at one point and they appeared to be fixed on me, but I knew they stared at nothing. His face was expressionless, and he was unaware of what was happening on this journey.

Then a caravan passing by brought back thoughts of Danny's former life. He was the youngest of eight children born to a Gypsy woman, and spent the first three months of his life in squalid conditions in a cramped caravan on a Gypsy site. When I first saw him in the casualty department, I felt a mixture of pity and revulsion. He was dressed in a dirty gray "baby grow," and he wore a blue knitted helmet, which, when removed, revealed his curly head of black hair encrusted in blood and vomit. His green eyes exuded yellow pus as he lay motionless. The events that led to his admission were never disclosed.

His parents were unable to account for any of his injuries, and they fled the country before any police inquiries. Because they had not visited or inquired about him since his admission, Danny was taken into the care of the local authorities. His injuries left him brain-damaged and blind.

The ambulance reached its destination, and I stepped down into the cold wintry chill. I enveloped Danny under my long black cloak as a bird would protect her young under her wing. The moment I dreaded had arrived. A rather pleasant lady met us and led us to the children's nursery, where I told her about

Danny's likes and dislikes. Then I handed Danny to her and hurried to the waiting ambulance, my tears beginning. Crying uncontrollably, I tried to hide my face from the ambulance driver, making some silly excuse about how the cold wind had made my eyes water. But I was sure he knew.

I often telephoned the children's home to inquire about Danny. Two years later he was adopted by a caring, childless couple.

Promises

SANDRA SMITH *Middletown, Ohio*

I watched an old nurse try to die last night.
I could hardly bare to hear
her hard breaths.

How many times did she stand with other nurses
watching this kind of pain,
make them swear to come in the night
with a lethal dose?

How many times was she sworn to that?

Over the oxygen mask
her eyes met mine.

These are the longest hours
when we face each other naked.
Both agonizing over promises made,
seldom kept.

Burnt-out Offerings

SANDRA SMITH *Middletown, Ohio*

We move like robots in our scorched skins,
pray no one notices
in the darkness of the night shift.

Registered by the state,
we give each other license
to bitch all night.

We have become
those old crusty nurses
we used to pity and avoid.

Sometimes I feel so crispy
I fear I will split
down the middle.

And whatever is left of my heart
will just blow away
as if it never mattered.

Bev Brown

SYBIL SMITH *Norwich, Vermont*

Bev Brown is immense, approaching freight-scale propor-
tions. It was I who, meanly, labeled her Jabba the Hut, but the
other nurses laughed, and the name stuck. It is not used, of
course, within her hearing.

Ridicule aside, I like Bev Brown. I am often assigned to her
when she comes in.

She needs a Psych admission two or three times a year. Last
week, as I took off my coat, I saw her name on the census board,
which hangs above the med cart at the nurses' station. Voice dis-
creetly pitched, I murmured to Elaine, another nurse, "Bev's
back?"

"Oh ayuh," said Elaine. "In all her muumuued glory."

Whenever Bev comes in she spends the first part of her ad-
mission supine in her room, draped in the tackiest of muumuus.
Cerise, ecru, chartreuse, cobalt, magenta; these are the hues her
massive frame is draped in. And the material? Orlon, rayon,
dacron: some slithery, shiny five-and-dime fabric. She lies in her
darkened room reeking of urine (she has a stress incontinence
problem), weeping, her right foot tapping like a human metro-
nome. She has Parkinson's disease. Sometimes it's her right
hand that moves (or foot and hand together) rasping rhythmic-
ally against the sheet, so that our pauses in conversation aren't
quite silent.

I got the scoop in report, of course. She didn't like her job as
a live-in nurse for a rich old woman. One of her sons was seri-
ously ill. The Department of Motor Vehicles was threatening to
take away her license. She couldn't take it anymore. Since she'd
been admitted yesterday, she'd refused pills, food, and water.
She wouldn't leave her room except to pee. It would have been
easier — and was, the first part of my shift — to leave her alone,
except for peeking in every hour or so.

But then came eight o'clock. Bev wouldn't take her meds.

"I don't need them," she muttered. Her back was to me, and
her voice was muffled by the pillows. I knew then that I'd have

to talk to her. I had the option of writing *patient refused* on the med sheet, but after all, this *was* my job. Some effort was required, and besides, I knew Bev. She could be coaxed.

I stared into the pill cup in my hand. "Clonopin," I said. "Sinemet, Colace, Imipramine, Ibuprofen. Come on, Bev, you take them all the time."

"I don't need them," she said, shifting in bed and releasing a balloon of scent. "What good are they?"

"What good are they? You know, Bev. You're an LPN."

Bev was silent, which, I suppose, I deserved, having deliberately misunderstood her. I put the pills on the bedside table and flopped into her chair. "Bev," I said, "it strikes me that you're not a happy camper."

"Brilliant," she replied.

I crossed my knees and worked the leather flat on my right foot free. Then I dangled it from my toes and admired my foot in the dim light that came through Bev's partially open door. "When you left last July, you were happy," I said. "What's been happening? I'm interested."

"My son is dying, for starters. And all Betsy ever does is ask for money. My Parkinson's is getting worse."

"How about that old lady you work for? How is that job going?"

"Crazy. You never know what she's gonna do next."

"What do you mean?"

And Bev was off and rolling. It had only taken a sum total of fifty words, spoken with a modicum of interest, to snag her. Like some massive, ornamental carp, she nosed up out of the dark bottom, toward the light. She likes to talk, is the thing. And she has a rough talent for description. She described the old lady so well I could almost hear her walker creaking through the dark halls of her fading, empty mansion, her almost defunct life. Bev does voices.

"Bev," she called in a witchy falsetto, "I have to go to the toilet." There was a pause, then, "Come quick, I have to do a big job!" Then, "Bev, what's that trash you're eating? I don't allow junk like that in my house." Then, "Bev, where are you going?" Bev's voice returned to normal and she did her own reply. "To Mars, if I'm lucky."

I laughed. "Your sense of humor is intact," I said. Bev likes to be told that. It's a point of pride with her. But even I could see that it was going to take more than a sense of humor to get her out of this one. She could watch reels of Charlie Chaplin and still be in the same boat, Norman Cousins notwithstanding.

As if reading my mind, Bev's shoulders started to shake. "Dr. Bentson's mad at me," she choked. "He asked me what I thought I was doing here this time."

"What did you say?"

"I told him I wanted to die in peace."

"But they won't let you die here," I pointed out. "People don't come to the hospital to die, unless they have terminal cancer or something."

"They can't make me eat," Bev said.

"If you keep refusing, they'll put an IV in your arm and a feeding tube down your nose."

"Hah," Bev snorted, to let me know what she thought of their puny tubes. Then she said, "If he sends me home I'll kill myself. I have enough medication to take out Burlington."

She said this with such relish that we both paused for awhile, savoring it. I could have pointed out that she was contradicting herself, but I didn't. I didn't want to hurt her dignity. Because she does have dignity. She sees herself as a tough customer, a hard-working, no-nonsense, kind-hearted woman.

She writes poems. She's shown them to me before. They are rife with misspelling but display a certain flair for metaphor. I remember, in particular, a poem to her father. Not the words, but what the words revealed. Her father started fucking her when she was fourteen. "You're a lot better at this than your mother," he told her.

She got pregnant. When she told whose it was, her mother beat her up and told the authorities she was a lying slut. She was sent to an unwed mother's home and gave the child up for adoption. After the home it was reform school, and then marriage to an abusive man. He was a construction worker and dragged his family from place to place. Bev had three more children and adopted three. Somewhere in there she got her LPN. I think that happened after her husband died — of drink. Does she miss her husband? *Hah!* That derisive *Hah* again. Fat chance. He could be hanging by the neck from that tree branch out there and she'd pull up a chair to enjoy the view.

I remember something else she told me about a tree. It was a very tall pine, down across the road, in the pasture. She would go there after her mother beat her. Her mother beat her more than she beat Bev's brother. The brother caved in, surrendered. But Bev fought back, would not submit. Her mother hit her so hard one time she broke her arm. Bev told the doctor she fell out of her tree.

She would leave the house and go down to that tree. She would climb into its topmost branches. She felt safe there. No one could touch her. She imagined she was closer to God. She saw that the world was bigger than her mother. When I start to care about Bev, I flash on that tree. I imagine her as she looks now, in a muumuu, at the very tippy top of a jack pine, gently swaying in the wind. Then I get afraid that it may break.

Somehow I had to convince her that life, in this case, was better than death, though I myself only half believed it. What was left for her after all? Her health problems were worsening. Her children had either done well and gone away, or done poorly and stayed nearby. She would end up in a nursing home herself, where the overworked aides would hate her for her weight, her shakiness.

"You're in a tough stretch, Bev," I began. "But no matter how bad life seems, you must have hope that things will get better."

Bev was quiet, listening. Invisible antennae waved around her head.

"You're a survivor, Bev. You know that. And it's because you like to do stuff. Like write poems and buy things for your grandchildren. Remember the last time you were here? You got so excited when you found a pair of shoes you could wear. Jogging shoes."

She was crying again. I could see her shoulders shaking. More words were needed. Alms for the poor. I had to go deeper.

And it *was* work. Because the sick aren't easy to love, nor the ugly. It's a discipline, like any other. Mother Teresa is an artist; her art, the acts of love she doles out ceaselessly.

I spoke to Bev of love and hope. I spoke to her of joy and goodness. I was a fountain of platitudes, which I hovered on the verge of believing. But occasionally an image came to me, of Bev at her medicine chest at home, gulping down pills with mouthfuls of chlorinated water. Or of Bev in the shower, dangling by her neck from the call bell. I began to entertain the logistics of the act, so to speak. There was an attraction there that I was afraid to let my heart explore. So I pushed the image away and talked on. And though one voice inside me said: *your words are crumbs, crusts, parings,* another voice said: *people can live on them. And do.*

Of course, Bev didn't spring from the bed, a new woman. She didn't flick on her light and do a jig. But she did turn toward me. It was a maneuver with many stages: a huffing, creaking re-arrangement of limbs. Her mousy short hair sprouted at various angles from her head. She reached for her eyeglasses on the bed-side table.

"Will you take your pills now?" I asked.

"Hand 'em over," she said. She downed the lot and chased it with water. "Thank you, Bev," I said.

She didn't reply.

"I'll be in to check on you later and talk some more. I have to give my other eight o'clocks."

Bev nodded. We had a deal now.

I left the room. I felt the way a diver must feel when he comes up too fast. Shivery. Disoriented. I went to the nurses' station. Elaine was there. She smiled at me.

"I'm an angel of mercy," I said.

"Florence Nightingale eat your heart out," she replied.

"I got Jabba to take her pills."

"Give the girl a merit raise."

"We're mean."

"But it's fun."

"You know, I was thinking something." I paused for a moment, to get it right. "When we make fun of the patients, it's like we're ducks on the shore, preening our feathers. We'd sink if we didn't."

Elaine laughed. "Not bad," she said, "as rationalizations go. Quite good actually." She closed the Land's End catalog she'd been flipping through and rose. "I'd love to stay and preen with you," she added, "but I've got to go float around in the milieu."

* * *

And the fact is, Bev did make it, again. I was off for a few days, and when I came back she was on a pass, shopping. When she returned she was bright-eyed and bushy-tailed. She showed me what she'd bought: mints for herself, sweatsuits for her grandchildren, and a journal with a spray of fall leaves encased in polyurethane on the front. I sat in her room with her and she bustled about, breathing heavily, handing me a mint. I suddenly thought of a poem I knew by Wallace Stevens. It's called "The Final Soliloquy of the Interior Paramour." I could only remember a few lines, but they stayed with me all evening.

> *It is in that thought that we collect ourselves,*
> *Out of all the indifferences, into one thing:*
>
> *Within a single thing, a single shawl*
> *Wrapped tightly round us, since we are poor . . .*

I thought Bev would have understood those lines.

Heroic Acts

JANET TRIPP *Minneapolis, Minnesota*

There is death here. There is also denial of death. Luz-Marie was brought to this country from Peru by her daughter at great expense after long and complicated arrangements. Since her stroke, her only evidence of awareness was to follow objects with her eyes. Last week she stopped doing that. The doctor wants to designate her DNR: Do Not Resuscitate. There is no hope of recovery. We would continue to ease the pain and keep her comfortable, but if her heart stopped, we wouldn't try to revive her. Her daughter can't accept what is inevitable and, to everyone but herself, obvious. She insists Luz-Marie be seen by a speech therapist. She will not allow a DNR sign to be placed on her mother's bed. Today, as her condition worsens, Luz-Marie is sent back to the hospital.

Rose, an LPN and a fifteen-year veteran here, is a part of my three-person team. On this day we progress down the corridor, caring for each patient in turn. In room 314 Eloise sits in her chair like a huge, pale Buddha, swollen with edema. She has no hair and breathes with difficulty. Her sister sits reading at her side. They exchange few words, but Eloise sleeps better when she is there. She won't talk with me about her cancer or dying, only about her failing eyesight. She doesn't want to go blind, she tells me. What she won't tell me is that she doesn't want to die.

Eloise is depressed, her sisters say. She feels her doctor has abandoned her. He doesn't come to see her on his weekly rounds. He no longer shows a concern for her. Erroneously, he thinks she doesn't need him now that he can't provide a cure. He doesn't understand. On this unit we don't cure people. We care for them.

In the next room are 91-year-old Dodie and her daughters. They've taken care of Mama for years, the three of them together. Dorothy has a job outside the home. June stays home with Mama. "Junie! Junie!" Mama cries whenever we turn her. "Now, Mama, it's all right." They pat her tenderly, ask for little kisses, tell us Mama's routine. We've broken that routine, and they can't care for her the way they want. They never talk about her dying. Mama will always be there to care for.

Dodie lies on her side curled up like a fetus. Her eyes are closed. She swats us away from her, spits the medicine back at us. "Son-of-a-bitch," she mutters as we turn her. "Oh Mama, stop that!" Junie says. Then to us, "She is never like this at home. So sweet and good tempered. Oatmeal and a doughnut for breakfast, and her coffee. She loves her coffee."

* * *

Evenings are my regular shift, but today I come in early for a staff meeting. It has been four days since I've worked, and Rose fills me in on the patients. She tells me Eloise is very bad. She is failing and afraid she will die alone. Dodie died during my evenings off. Her daughters denied she was dead until the mortician came. They tried to get the nurses to start an IV; they couldn't let her go. She was their mother. She was their child.

As the meeting begins, the night nurse tells about her favorite patient, Sam, who died last night. She found him already blue and stiff. "I rolled him over and called his name," she says. "He sighed a couple of times, so even then I wasn't sure. I thought he was dead. Usually, I know."

If we're with our patients when they die, we've done our work. If they die alone, we feel ashamed, guilty, sad. We can not die with them or for them, but it helps to hold a hand. It helps us both.

The chaplain leads the meeting and we talk about the things we take home from work stuck in our throats and in our heads. It clears the air and lifts the burdens. The meeting ends and we go back to work.

* * *

Now it is Eloise whose time has come. Her huge belly lies stone-heavy. Two of us can't slide her up in bed. Her liver is immense from the cancer; her abdomen, swollen huge with fluid. Her legs are like sausages, the skin bloodless and soggy. After the chemotherapy her hair is just beginning to grow back. A white stubble covers her head and whiskers circle her mouth. Her forehead has a pearly-grainy coating. She vomits the little she can drink. No longer can she sip through a straw. "That took the sap right out of me," her sister says when she sees it. Eloise sits leaning to one side, her head on her chest, her breath shallow.

Her sister comes out in the hall to ask, "Is this Cheyne-Stokes breathing? Is this the end?" Not yet. Poor Eloise isn't released yet. She lies there chained to her heart that pumps and pumps and pumps.

Eloise is actively dying. Before I came here I hadn't realized what hard work it can be. With the increased pain we only turn her once a shift. We come out of her room crying. "Don't ever lose that," Rose tells the newly graduated nurse who is wiping her tears away. "If we didn't feel, we would be no good to them."

"Today," Eloise's sister says, "my daughter asked, Will Auntie get well and bake Christmas cookies with me this year? What can I say? It breaks my heart. Last year she spent an afternoon with each child baking cookies."

"What a gift she gave them," I reply, thinking of my dad and the times he and my youngest son, Jonathan, had gone shopping together. Gifts of ourselves, of our time, that is really all we have of value to give to one another.

* * *

Families pillow the dying's pain. I watch them walking up the hall—whole families with nieces and nephews and shirttail cousins bearing gifts. Chin Lee's family carries many-tiered silver temples of food. Enticing foreign smells waft behind as they pass down the long hall.

I see that when the families come, the sick ones smile. Their voices grow stronger. They gather their strength to sit up. They rest easier. Some do get better and go home, even from here. We will probably cure Chin Lee. She was admitted to Chesterfield with osteomyelitis, a bone infection. In Cambodia she buried eight children before coming to Minnesota. Five were killed, she says, by the communists. They came to her door one night and killed her husband and the children. She is here now with two grown children who had escaped. Her children and grandchildren come in long lines of smiling, cordial faces.

I can't imagine, when I try, delivering, nurturing, loving, worrying over eight children and then losing them. Eight. I look at her and recognize my error. I hold life's joys too tightly, not accepting the inevitable pain, but looking on it as an undeserved affront, indignant that illness should happen to me, horrified that my loved ones ever die. In loving, loss is inevitable.

When I left work last week I went in to say good-bye to Eloise. I was sure she would be gone when I returned today. She is still here. Barely conscious now, she grimaces when we turn her. Rose asks, "Are you in pain?" She is unable to speak. She mouths the word no. That is all.

I imagine myself in her place. So this is what dying can be like. "I can do this," I tell myself. I can contain this pain and this knowledge. It is difficult to consider for long, and I busy myself arranging her covers.

One evening when she was stronger, Eloise had said to me, "It isn't hard to think about death when you're young and it is far away. It isn't as easy now that I see it coming."

I quicken my pace. I'm getting behind schedule, and there is medicine to give out, new patients to tend, acts of heroism to witness. I've learned some things in this place. We don't get to choose much about our dying in the usual run of things. Even in our dying, we can't be fully in the moment, constantly aware that this is it. Now I die. We cannot look straight at the sun for long. We shield our eyes momentarily and then steal another look not to be blinded by the brilliance.

From the Diary of a Clinic Nurse, Poland, 1945

BELLE WARING *Washington, D.C.*

The only safe conclusion to be drawn from the multitude of reports is that
life in dark closets, wolves' dens, forests or sadistic parents' backyards is not
conducive to good health and normal development.
   Eric H. Lenneberg on wolf children in *The Genesis of Language*,
   eds. Frank Smith and George A. Miller

The linguists will use her to theorize on the origins of speech —
of which she now has none. I'd like to bathe her without being
flayed by her six-year-old teeth.

Female child found abandoned in thick woods, healthy but feral,
feet indurated. Hearing intact.

Bays like a wolf.

When I speak, her eyes turn curious. Even dogs grasp simple
commands, and she is, a priori, more intelligent than they.
Marie, I call her, after Curie, who took two Nobels, chemistry
and physics.

The doctors note her Jewish traits: deep-hooded eyes. Semitic
arch, hair black whorls reduced now to a bramble mat half down
her back. To save her from the camps, someone must have led
her deep into the woods to wander there like Gretel. Like
Snow White.

Doctor Krynski tells his students how Rome's founders were
brothers suckled by a wolf.

But this girl isn't founding Rome.

Red Army men brought her in this week, naked under the
sergeant's coat. At least they hadn't raped — still, her howls
raised the hair on my neck.

Marie, I say, and she looks at me as if the syllables meant something.

Start with the resonant consonant, *M*—nasal passage open, mouth blocked. Lips meet, then release. *Muh. Marie.*

Dirty Jew, the night nurse says, right to her face. She hears the tone, growls back, and spits. The psychiatrist orders chloral hydrate, and when she wakes up scrubbed and shorn like Samson, her eyes say, Thou hast betrayed me.

Yes, I envy her those maternal wolves who kill only to eat, not like the Nazis who shot my brothers, the Red Army men who sat smug across the river and looked on as Warsaw was slaughtered.

My studies in physics have been blasted of course, and now the doctors snap at me as if I were their serf tending pigs.

But I am not a simple nurse.

Alone with the child, I lay down to bare my neck like a dog surrendering, and for the first time she crouched near enough to sniff me. Then the neurologist barged in and, finding us on the floor like that, had a jealous snit. The grunting little academic — he wants her for research, but first he must examine her — and this she won't permit. He'd have to drug her — and drugged, she won't react. So he slammed out.

I gave her an orange whirligig, I swear I heard her laugh: a hoarse, exotic yelp.

Muh, I said, *Marie.*

I lay on the floor like a pup at play. I lay there and begged the Blessed Virgin for Her help and was seized quite suddenly with weeping. The child fixed me with a concentrated stare, then crawled over and sniffed my hand: carbolic soap and tears, if indeed these have a scent.

The doctors came, and she fled then to her corner as they shouted at my lack of dignity. I need the work. I did not shout back.

Marie. You see me, how I'll soon turn twenty-three and have no sweetheart, family dead, mind matted up and useless. I am scared for you, rescued now from woods so thick no one heard you shriek. I have never seen your maternal wolves, but I've heard them howling at the brash, callipygous moon, wolves snagged down here in this wrong life. Wrong continent. Wrong earth.

From the Diary of a Prisoner's Nurse, Mississippi, 1972

BELLE WARING *Washington, D.C.*

We had her open into the uterus, down to the bag of waters,
which was (God knows how) still intact around the baby —
floating, oblivious, asleep.

                             Oh! The surgeon said. I had never
heard one of his kind sound so innocent, surprised. Never seen
the womb laid open to a fetus sleeping head-up in its home —

translucent sac. But you can't stand around all night
like Biblical shepherds, dumb with adoration. The surgeon has
to shred the bag — glistening surgical birth. Now

go back
to the bag of waters and its cloudy light, silvery mizzle
like March rain at midday and the light way back behind it.

Light in prison can be like that, skim, before sunup,
gray to bluish where they found her in labor, tetanic con-
    tractions,
the uterine muscle stretched morbidly thin, the baby

breech, head palpable as a cat under an old quilt, something
wrong, her first baby, the girl screaming and the inmates, louder,
screaming over her, *Get the doctor!*

Uterine rupture. A basket splitting from the weight of its fruit.
She was twenty-one. Wheat. Wax. Dust. How we got the kid out
I don't know — the surgeon was slow as an old cur.

She just bled out.
                After, the surgeon offered me a smoke,
which I took to avoid letting him catch me in the eye.

The eyes of the dying sometimes glaze over like cloudy plastic
stretched over a window to thwart the rain — the film of it
fuzzes the light. The old eyes of the scrub nurse, eyes over the
   mask,

sad cynic: *Give it up.* They didn't try to save the mother.
One year out of school, I would not obey, went for the anesthe-
   sia cart,
albumin in drawer three —

                              then her pressure — the bottom
                              dropped out.
Couldn't get her back. The baby screamed at birth.
The baby screamed at birth.

Twenty-four-week Preemie, Change of Shift

BELLE WARING *Washington, D.C.*

We're running out of O_2
screaming down the southwest freeway in the rain
the nurse practitioner and me
rocking around in the back of an ambulance
trying to ventilate a preemie with junk for lungs
when we hit
rush hour

    Get us the hell out of here

You bet the driver said and pulled right onto the median strip
with that maniacal glee they get

I was too scared for the kid and drunk with the speed
the danger — that didn't feel like danger at all
it felt like love — to worry about *my* life
Fuck that

Get us back to Children's so we can put a chest tube in this kid

And when we got to the unit
the attending physician — Loretta — was there
and the nurses
and the residents
they save us
Loretta plants her stethoscope on the kid's chest
and here comes the tech driving the portable X-ray
like it's a Porsche — *Ah Jesus* he says
the baby's so puny he could fit on your dinner plate

X-ray says the tech
and everybody backs up, way back
except for Loretta
so the tech drapes a lead shield over her chest

X-ray says the tech

There's a moment after he cones down the lens
just before he shoots
you hold your breath, you forget
what's waiting
back at your house

Nobody blinks
poised for that sound that radiological
meep

and Loretta with her scrub top on backwards
so you can't peep down to her peanutty boobs
Loretta with her half-Chinese, half-Trinidadian
half-smile
Loretta, all right, ambu-bagging the kid
never misses a beat
calm and sharp as a mama-cat who's kicked the dog's butt
now softjaws her kitten out of the ditch

There's a moment
you can't even hear the bag
puffing
quick quick quick
before the tech shoots
for just that second
I quit being scared
I forget to be scared

God

How can people abandon each other?

Baby Random

BELLE WARING *Washington, D.C.*

tries a nose-dive, kamikaze,
when the intern flings open the isolette.

The kid almost hits the floor. I can see the headline:
DOC DUMPS TOT. Nice save, nurse.

Why thanks. Young physician: "We have to change
the tube." His voice trembles, six weeks

out of school. I tell him: "Keep it to a handshake,
you'll be OK." Our team resuscitated

this Baby Random, birthweight
one pound, eyelids still fused. Mother's

a junkie with HIV. Never named him.
Where I work we bring back terminal preemies,

No Fetus Can Beat Us. That's our motto. I have
a friend who was thrown into prison. Where do birds

go when they die? Neruda wanted to know. Crows
eat them. Bird heaven? Imagine the racket.

When Random cries, petite fish on shore, nothing
squeaks past the tube down his pipe. His ventilator's

a high-tech bellows that kicks in & out. Not
up to the nurses. Quiet: a pigeon's outside,

color of graham crackers, throat oil on a wet street,
wings spattered white, perched out of the rain.

I have friends who were thrown in prison, Latin
American. Tortured. Exiled. Some people have

courage. Some people have heart. *Corazon.*
After a shift like tonight, I have the usual

bad dreams. Some days I avoid my reflection in store
windows. I just don't want anyone to look at me.

Euthanasia

BELLE WARING *Washington, D.C.*

Two milligrams of morphine in the IV. He just went to sleep, she said.

Top of the shift and she tells me she killed a kid.

Says it under her breath, bedside, in neonatal intensive care, the room blown open with noise and flurry and light — ventilators snap and blow, monitors glimmer with QRS-respiration-&-pressure, IVs tick, computers clack STAT lab reports, chest tubes boil, mordant alarms drive everyone nuts, beepers nag, telephones spaz off the hook, ward clerks run interference, parents visit or just sit — stunned — knots of doctors confer and work under pitiless banks of fluorescent lights — a hospital spaceship. And us, the nurses, at warming tables, isolettes — preemies inside.

Watch her eyes, the pocked gray moons. Just hitting her — she killed a kid.

You told anyone about this?

No, she said.

Her whispering face — long nose of the Scots, wry mouth of the Irish. Rusty hair. Intelligent.

Nobody? You told a priest?

She said, *I haven't been to confession in years.*

You going now?

Didn't hesitate. *No,* she said.

Time plays with your mistakes and bulks up your regrets. She
didn't know that. Eleven years younger than I.

I was sick of them sticking that baby, she said.

Who wasn't. Baby No Code — Do Not Resuscitate. 440 grams,
down to 380. Hopeless, needled, threaded, trussed, never left to
rest. Eyes still fused, and his skin — the skin of water breaking
under your touch.

He needed to die, she said.

I knew her family — Irish Catholic, like my father — unlike my
mother, atheist by default.

Look at this kid — ready for school, I said, glad to be minding a
three-pounder on the mend, mewing to be fed.

I was avoiding the argument.

Before *Roe v. Wade,* I'd see girls come in the ER with the tire
irons up them. With the Drano douches. You get a bellyful of
that. I would not go back to that.

So I was older and she was green, but still a good nurse with the
sickest kids. Not hard to needle an IV port. Put a kid down like
a sick cat.

What if it got routine. Watch her eyes. Ashy moons. Scared,
explaining herself.

They were using him for IV practice, she said.

I tell you she's a good nurse, resourceful and quick, none of the
smarmy perkiness some use to keep the carnage at a distance.
She'll keep a bumbling resident from harming a kid.

Yet. Some doctors, well trained and blessed with their own
intuition, aren't wrong at all. And she needs always to be right.

What about a case that's not clear-cut—a kid who defies intrauterine insult, medical fuckup, nursing blunder, equipment failure, intracranial hemorrhage, infection, and the dysfunction of every one of its puny organs. Kid who fights like a mad dog, who fools us, lives and thrives for no goddamn good reason we can name.

He needed to die, she said.

But did you need to kill him? I bundled the three-pounder and put him in her arms. *Feed this kid for me. I need a smoke.*

She was a good nurse. I tell you the truth.

No problem, she said.

Between Rounds

BELLE WARING *Washington, D.C.*

That experimental chemo—I knew
it wouldn't work. I said Baby, I'd never let them
do this to me.
             He shot back—if you had what I had
you'd take whatever they threw at you.
                                    So

he took it. The IV ticked
right into his blood and his hair
fell out in clumps like down. Andy, you knew

your brother, how he stared like a saint in a Byzantine
icon. Eyes of Jeremiah. Even if he did scorn
God. I'm afraid

to tell you this. The room twisted down
dark around his bed and then light
pulsed out of him and grew and kept
growing. Sweet Christ I was
scared. We were going away
from the world. Terminus.
                        You knew
your brother, you were the one who lay
under the piano while he played. His music
soaked into the fissures that words never
touch. And we never
taped any of it. It's here now
here in our bones. I'm not

explaining anything. The nurse
breezed in to check his temp. His eyes
opened like a wet newborn—that tender.

Surprised at having passed through a wall.

I Couldn't Touch the Wall

ELLEN DIDERICH ZIMMER *Elizabeth, Arkansas*

My sisters, I've come to the wall.
It's long and black and shiny.
It's frightening. It envelops me.
It's been many, many years,
    Too many years.
I've hidden you, Vietnam, deep within me.
The wall makes me remember you. I was there.

My sisters, I took a picture of the wall,
    a picture too, of the birthday cake,
    the medal, the letter, the opened bottle
    of whiskey, lying at the base of the wall.
I held my camera and took more pictures.

I saw a brother, who knelt, with
    an arm outstretched, to
    touch his long-lost friend,
    a name engraved on the wall.

My heart so heavy, my feet so weak.
I walked on, I became so weary . . .

My sisters, I've come to the wall, but
I couldn't touch it. Although I wanted to.
It's too far to reach. I might feel them.

I know they're there,
    I can hear them crying,
    I think they're still bleeding.

Oh, my brothers, with all my heart,
    so many years ago, I comforted and cared,
    but it wasn't enough.

How horrible of me,
I can't even remember your names.
You, who died in my arms,
I, who listened to your last words.
I've enclosed you, you're buried within me.

I'll be back, my brothers, I'll be back
to touch the wall, when I can gather the strength.

It's a first step . . .
Welcome home, my Sisters!

Afterword

CORTNEY DAVIS & JUDY SCHAEFER

Creating a Sacred Space

For several years I've been listening with admiration as the poetry and fiction of physicians has, more and more, been presented at readings and in medical and creative writing journals. John Stone, Richard Selzer, Alice Jones, Jon Mukand, Raphael Campo, and so many others write bravely about their work—and readers, most of whom will at some time be patients, have responded with fascination. *So this is what my doctors are thinking!* I've praised the doctors for their candor, and yet I've been angry too. When they told of struggles to combat death and illness, of those moments when they felt a sudden, compassionate connection to their patients, a connection most of them had not been trained to seek and were surprised to find, I couldn't help thinking, *This is nothing new to nurses. We have felt this connection, this empathy since ancient times!* And yet, the nurses were silent. I wondered, where are the nurses' stories?

* * *

Jane (the name could as well be Kamiko or Larry) casts off her stethoscope, takes a pen and pad and begins to write. Her patient, Mr. Hererra, died today. Jane was alone in the room with him—the physician had left, saying the outcome was inevitable, and the family lived too far away—so Jane held his hand and waited, as Mr. Hererra did, for death. Every death reminds Jane of every other death she's ever seen. Her mother's. Her friends.' All those patients. Now she wants to record this event while the details are vivid in her mind's eye: the way his skin changed, the way his eyes seemed to empty. Jane wants passionately *to remember.* Maybe she doesn't articulate this, but if she can remember this patient, if she can bear witness to his individual struggle, then every life will have significance. Her patients' lives. Her mother's. Her own.

Nurses are often alone with their patients, creating a sacred space. Picture the bed with a patient in it, a patient in pain or perhaps simply afraid. See the nurse next to the bed. He or she may be involved with some technical problem: the malfunctioning ventilator, the insistent warning bell on the IV. Or she may be doing the work of listening, of comforting, *of staying*. Unlike the doctor, she will come and go a hundred times a shift to this patient. And she will walk, again and again in one day, beside death, beside birth and pain—sometimes like a shadow, more often like a partner. What the nurse knows and experiences as a caregiver is different from what the doctor knows, different from what the family experiences. The nurse descends and returns from hell; she also sees grace.

When Judy Schaefer and I met, we recognized a common bond at once, a shared vision. And so, eventually, the idea for this anthology was born. The work has been joyful, and a family has been created—an international, diverse community of registered nurses who write honestly about their work. The response to our call for submissions was overwhelming. Word spread from nurse to nurse, notices appeared on the Internet, magazines half a world away ran the story of our search. Fat envelopes appeared in our mailboxes: nurses were saying what had never been said before.

Some of the nurses in this collection have never been published, in fact, have never dreamed of publishing. Many, like eighty-three-year-old Adele Sarrazin, took a chance and trusted that Judy and I would carefully read work that, until now, had often been private. Some are nationally recognized writers but have often kept the nursing poems, the nursing stories, apart from their other work. It's almost as if we've all been waiting, hoping perhaps that what we do is so well understood it doesn't need explication. Maybe too we've been afraid to say that we don't always love our work or our patients, and that we can be worn down by illness, death, or by the still-too-often subservient position of nurse-is-to-doctor as squire-is-to-knight. Sometimes, we can't bear to write our stories because we've been too moved and feel too fragile.

But all nurses who write have something in common. When we write about our work, we re-create that sacred space, draw again the shimmering line around patient and nurse, draw them together. By revealing the details, the *dailiness* of nursing, we discover, and then can teach others, universal truths about life and death. Just as we know the feel of our hands on the patient's body, we have learned these truths by heart.

Thank you to Judy Schaefer for her constant good cheer and love for what nurses have to say. I'm indebted to my husband, Jon, for his support; to the nurses whose brave words have created this collection; and to Joanne Trautmann Banks whose foreword gracefully sets the stage for our sacred space.

We are an ancient tribe, we nurses — and, like other ancient tribes whose stories and myths last from generation to generation, we must pass on what we know to survive.

C. D.

Expanding the Language

It has been my wish, for as long as I have been a nurse, to know what other nurses think. Curiosity about human beings — how they work and think — led me to nursing in the first place. Yet, I wanted to know more. I wanted to know more about these fascinating creatures with whom I worked side by side. Nurses are more often the task *doers* than the philosophy *makers*. I wanted to hear their philosophies: the thoughts wherein they lingered and mulled over the events of their days.

A shared vision of nursing and literature was apparent in my first conversation with Cortney Davis. We both articulated from our gut, heart, and spirit how our poetry enhanced our nursing practice. We would not back down from this conviction that nurses have something important to say, and that saying it will expand the practice of nursing and the practice of language. I read Cortney's "Nurse as Angel of Mercy" (*Literature and Medicine*, Spring 1992) and knew immediately a comrade of words and wards. This conviction and the resulting search for nursing's voice has been at the heart of this anthology.

This is the beginning of a new tradition in literature. Imagine the group of forty-nine nurses published in this book, gathered around night-shift-old coffee from a rancid pot, sipping, talking, and creating words to explain our joy and our pain. Each nurse in this collection represents thousands more. Nurses have the rare privilege to be there in those seconds when the patient takes a turn for the worse or a turn for the better. This privilege is repeated more times in one shift than can ever be fully acknowledged. Jeanne LeVasseur's "Lullaby" reminds us of those moments of immense human depth that insert themselves without warning into the workday. The writer-nurse and the reader are changed. Nursing and language have then reached the level of art.

In addition, the literary tools of metaphor, allegory, and symbol have long been nursing tools. The art of nursing can be enhanced and expanded by the use of these devices, as demonstrated in this volume. Likewise, the language will expand as nurses contribute in a formal way that allows a reader to return again and again to the volume pulled down from the shelf. This anthology offers voices that the reader may never have heard before.

The number and quality of submissions we received was overwhelming. If I have ever desired to know what nurses were thinking, I learned quickly. It was an early morning in the spring when I sat on my front porch at the foot of the Blue Mountains in Pennsylvania. I sat down with a cup of freshly made coffee and the first batch of submissions. I read, I laughed, and I wept. Nurses with strong convictions and so much to say! Until that morning I had not seen the robin that had taken up residence in our blue spruce. As I read, the intense robin went back and forth with worms, back and forth to the fledglings. As I read, I felt like a fledgling. I remember reading Michael Kelly's "Why I Went into Nursing" that spring morning. I chuckled and stretched in the morning sun and felt nourished by my feeling of recognition.

Thank you to Cortney Davis, a highly focused coeditor, for sharing the vision and her energy. Thank you to Jo Banks for believing in us. A special thank you to Larry and Jane Kienle, the Kienle Center, and to "Teddy" Graham for many years of encouragement. Thank you to my daughter Jill Lenhardt for sharing her knowledge of art history and her skilled vision, and thank you to my husband, Dan, for being there.

To the nurses who sent us all those bulging envelopes — thank you! I am glad to be a nurse. Together we have expanded the body of knowledge of nursing and language.

J. S.

Joanne Trautmann Banks became the first full-time professor of literature in a medical school when she was appointed to the Pennsylvania State University College of Medicine in 1972. Over the years, her writing has brought the methodologies of the arts to the practical benefit of medicine and the insights of medicine to the illumination of literature. She is founder of the journal *Literature and Medicine*, and the coeditor, with Nigel Nicolson, of the six-volume *Letters of Virginia Woolf* (Harcourt Brace Jovanovich, 1975–80).

Carolyn Barbier works as a registered nurse and lives in New Mexico with her husband, cat, and parrot. After two of her closest friends each fought against the wishes of the attending physicians to allow a loved one to die, Carolyn wrote *Nighthawks* as a voice for those whose freedom to choose is not secure. "Life at any price is not an option for those who live passionately."

Jeanne Beall, a registered nurse, was born and raised in Baltimore, Maryland. She lives in Idaho with her husband and two children. Her poetry has been published in several regional journals.

Janet Bernichon is an emergency room nurse on Long Island. Her short stories and poems appear in *Blue Unicorn, Bogg, Chiron Review, Olympia Review*, and other journals. Janet's work also appears in many of the e-zines on the Internet.

Kaija Blalock lives, writes, and works as a registered nurse in the Washington, D.C., metropolitan area. Her work has appeared in *Original Sin*.

Geoffrey Bowe was born in the English Lake District in 1957 and qualified as a registered nurse in 1983. His poems have been published in *Nursing Standard* and in an anthology of South Eastern (English) Poetry by *Poetry Now*. He works in an orthopedic ward in Kent, England.

Carol Brendsel completed her nursing education in Philadelphia in 1967 and thereafter headed for San Francisco. After a profound experience in childbirth, she became a practicing homebirth midwife; currently, she works as an obstetrical nurse in labor and delivery. She is inspired by both her vocation and avocation.

Ruth E. Brooks was born in New York City in 1938 and is a 1960 graduate of Harlem Hospital School of Nursing. In addition, she holds certification in editing from Georgetown University. Married with one son and one grandchild, she works as a psychiatric nurse in Washington, D.C.

Celia Brown, a registered nurse, grew up in County Mayo, Ireland, arriving in the United States in the sixties. She completed the M.A. at Dartmouth College with a collection of poems, *Blue Ambition*. Her work has appeared in journals including *Maryland Poetry Review, Seattle Review, Visions International, Federal Poet, Salmon, Penumbra, Dartmouth Medicine,* and *Irish Echo.* She recently read her poetry at the Library of Congress.

Jeanne Bryner is an emergency room nurse. Her poems have appeared in several magazines, including *A Gathering of Poets, Negative Capability, Prairie Schooner, Journal of Emergency Nursing, Journal of Holistic Medicine, Journal of Emergency Medicine, Poetry East,* and in the anthology, *What's Become of Eden: The Family at Century's End* (Slapering Hol Press, 1994). She received a Pushcart Prize nomination in 1994. Her chapbook, *Breathless,* will be published by Kent State University Press.

Richard Callin has poems published in various magazines including *Black Warrior Review, Plum Review, Spoon River Poetry Review,* and *Journal of the American Medical Association.* He works for a visiting nurse and hospice organization in California.

Sarah Collings is a critical care nurse in Bridgeport, Connecticut, and an avid horsewoman. She holds an M.F.A. in creative writing from Columbia University and has published poetry in *Western Journal of Medicine,* and articles in the *New York Times* and *American Journal of Nursing.* She has illustrated a children's book that her mother wrote.

Cortney Davis, an adult nurse practitioner currently working in women's health, is the author of *The Body Flute* (Adastra Press, 1994). Her poems have been published in *Calyx, Hudson Review, Ms., Crazyhorse, Journal of the American Medical Association, Literature and Medicine,* and other journals. She is the recipient of a 1994 National Endowment for the Arts fellowship in poetry and two poetry grants from the Connecticut Commission on the Arts. She lives in Connecticut with her husband, Jon, and has two married children, Lisa and Christopher.

Eva D. Deeb is a retired registered nurse living in Florida. She graduated from the Good Samaritan School of Nursing in 1944. Her short stories have been published in two anthologies from the Living Historian Writing Classes of Ocala, Florida: *World War II: We Look Back* (1992) and *Watermarks* (1993).

Theodore Deppe is the author of *Children of the Air* (Alice James Books, 1990). His work has appeared in journals such as *Kenyon Review, Massachusetts Review, Crazyhorse,* and others. He has received a National Endowment for the Arts fellowship in poetry, and a poetry grant from the Connecticut Commission on the Arts. He received his B.S.N. from Berea College and an M.F.A. in Writing from Vermont College. Presently he works on a psychiatric unit for children and as a creative writing teacher in a high school for the arts.

Elizabeth Desimone, a family nurse practitioner, served as a missionary nurse in Guatemala from 1977–1980. "The Gift: La Cumbre, Guatemala," is taken from her book *Guatemala in My Blood*, for which she received a grant from the Seattle Arts Commission. Her features and articles have appeared in regional newspapers.

R. Eric Doerfler is a registered nurse and homeopath in Pennsylvania. His poems have been published in *Samizdat, Patterson Literary Review, Tabula Rasa*, and *Wildwood Journal*. He has completed his first novel, *Excalibur, Rise!*

Jane Farrell is a retired registered nurse and nursing author. She has published three volumes of poetry and contributes regularly to a number of small journals. In addition to publishing widely in nursing journals between 1974 and 1985, she has authored two nursing textbooks, *Illustrated Guide to Orthopedic Nursing* (J. B. Lippincott, 1977, 1982, 1986) and *Nursing Care of the Older Person* (J. B. Lippincott, 1990).

Helen Trubek Glenn received a B.S. and R.N. degree from Cornell in 1961. At midlife she began writing poetry and graduated from Vermont College's M.F.A. in Writing program in 1991. Her poems have appeared in *Yankee, Poet Lore, Spoon River Quarterly, Northeast*, and other magazines.

Christine Grant is an assistant professor of Psychiatric Mental Health Nursing in Pennsylvania. Dr. Grant also works in private practice, where she treats victims of rape and battering. Her poems have appeared in *Lyrical Iowa*, and she has published clinical articles focusing on issues of interpersonal violence. She is qualified as an expert witness in many courts.

Amy Haddad is a registered nurse who specializes in applied ethics education in all areas of healthcare. She became interested in poetry and short stories as a vehicle to teach ethics and to express her own experiences in hospice and homecare.

Mitzi Higley is a nurse educator in Tennessee. Penning poems has been a lifelong pleasure. Her poems present themselves to her nearly in full, and she rarely shares them. "They are from the privacy of my soul."

Nina Howes is a registered nurse and a political activist who loves acting, dancing, and writing. As an actress, she has performed in regional, off, and off-off Broadway productions. She has an article, "Nature Boy," forthcoming in an anthology about autistic children.

Georgiana Johnson graduated from a diploma program in 1969 and went on to earn a B.S. in psychology and an M. Ed. in health education from Penn State University. Currently a school nurse working with a high-school population, she has worked in a variety of settings including medical-surgical, inpatient drug and alcohol, and home health. She lives with her husband in a 100-year-old farmhouse with their Rottweiler and two cats. This is her first submitted work.

Michael Kelly practices in the area of home healthcare and hospital staff relief. He recently became an EMT. He has published half a dozen books of poetry and has been frequently anthologized. After graduating from the University of New Mexico, Michael taught before entering nursing.

Angela Kennedy is a registered general nurse living in Essex, England. She began writing as a student nurse and has contributed to many journals and magazines in the British nursing, feminist, and socialist press. She is currently editing a book about reproductive politics. She is married with two children.

Shirley Kobar is a registered nurse working in Denver and living in Aurora, Colorado, with her two children and a supportive husband. Nursing has always been an important part of her life. She has poems published in *Array*, *Climbing Art*, and *Trail and Timberline*.

Jeanne LeVasseur is a nurse practitioner and a university School of Nursing faculty member. She holds an M.F.A. in Writing from Vermont College and has poems published in *Embers*, *Haight-Ashbury Literary Journal*, *Literature and Medicine*, *Nimrod*, *South Coast Poetry Journal*, *Spoon River Poetry Review*, *Yankee*, and other magazines.

Patricia Maher is a gerontological nurse practitioner in Cambridge, Massachusetts. She received her B.S.N. from Boston College in 1975 and her M.S. in 1981 from Boston University. She has worked in homecare for fifteen years, and she began to write poems from her nursing experience a few years ago.

Veneta Masson is a family nurse practitioner and the director of a small clinic in inner-city Washington, D.C. A poet and essayist, her chapbook, *Just Who*, is available through the National League for Nursing. Her poems have been published as well in *Nursing Spectrum*, *Nursing Outlook*, and *Journal of Christian Nursing*.

Lianne Elizabeth Mercer works as a shift supervisor at a psychiatric hospital in San Antonio, Texas. Her chapbook, *No Limits But*

Light, was published in October 1994 by Chili Verde Press. Her short stories and poems have appeared in several anthologies and literary magazines. She is studying to become a poetry therapist.

Muriel Murch is a registered nurse, writer, and radio programmer. Her book, *Journey in the Middle of the Road*, is forthcoming from Sibyl Publications in Oregon. Currently, she is writing a collection of short stories and producing "Living with Literature" for the department of drama and literature of KPFA Radio. For the past twenty-two years she has lived, worked, and raised her family on a small farm in northern California.

Madeleine Mysko served as an Army Nurse at the famed burn unit of Brooke Army Medical Center during the Vietnam War. She is a recent graduate of the Writing Seminars of Johns Hopkins University. Her poems and fiction have appeared most recently in *Christian Century*, *Southern Humanities Review*, and *Hudson Review*.

Leslie Nyman has been a registered nurse since 1978. She works for an HMO in Western Massachusetts as a health educator. Her publications include a short story in the anthology *If I Had My Life to Live Over, I Would Pick More Daisies* (Papier-Mache Press, 1992).

Dawn Ramm is a home health nurse working for a large HMO in Vallejo, California. She enjoys being a grandmother, traveling, tai chi, and poetry. She has poems appearing in *Ruah* and *Mediphors*.

Joyce Renwick was a registered nurse and an independent fiction consultant in Iowa City, Iowa. Before graduating from the University of Iowa Writers' Workshop, she worked in orthopedic trauma. Her fiction has appeared in *Southern Review*, *Alaska Quarterly Review*, *Folio*, *Michigan Quarterly Review*, and elsewhere, and has been anthologized in *Finding Courage: Writings by Women* (Crossing Press, 1989), *Best American Short Stories* (Houghton Mifflin, 1982), and *Revelation and Other Fiction from the Sewanee Review* (Harmony House, 1992). She taught fiction workshops at the Iowa Summer Writing Festival and was a contributing editor to *Mediphors*. Tragically, Joyce died in a car accident as this anthology was going to press.

Debra J. Sandy is a registered nurse who practices in an inpatient research center with a large oncology population in Madison, Wisconsin. Her nursing experience includes cardiac/trauma/surgical intensive care and oncology, in which she has been a staff nurse as well as a manager. Debra has worked for the majority of her 20-year career as a night nurse, where she is able to spend some very special time with her patients.

Adele Germaine Sarrazin is an 83-year-old retired registered nurse, who chose to raise her four children at home and return to nursing when they were in school. As a nurse on maternity in a small, eleven-bed hospital, there were many nights when she had time to write and to study Spanish. Adele has been legally blind for three years.

Judy Schaefer is a registered nurse certified in pediatrics. A native of St. Louis, Missouri, she now lives in Pennsylvania with her husband, Dan, an avid outdoorsman. She is an active staff member of the magazines *Wild Onions* and *Mediphors*. She is a member of the Kienle Center for Humanistic Medicine, Society for Health and Human Values, and is on the board of the Pennsylvania Nurses Association, South-central Pennsylvania. She is the eastern United States customer service manager for a global organization that provides chronic disease home services and management. She will complete her M.A. in Literature in 1995.

Elsie Schmied is retired after working for over forty years as a registered nurse in a variety of positions and in four states. Her publications, *Maintaining Cost Effectiveness* (1979) and *Organizing for Care* (1982) were seminal works in nursing. She now writes poetry and short stories for small mainstream periodicals, writes a weekly book review, and is working on her second novel.

Bethany Schroeder is a registered nurse who also holds M.S. and M.F.A. degrees, studying nursing at the College of the Desert and San Jose State University, and English literature and poetry at University of California at Riverside and Cornell University. She is the staff development coordinator for a homecare and hospice service in Mountain View, California, and is an advisor and writer for *Nurseweek*. Her poems have appeared in a variety of small-press journals.

Ellen Shay is an adult critical care nurse who has worked in Seattle and New York City, as well as on an acute psychiatric unit in White Plains, New York. She has been writing short pieces for years, and this is her first submitted work. She is currently busy parenting two small children with her husband, Ted, in Palo Alto, California. In addition to writing, she enjoys rock climbing, body building, dancing, and reading the Sunday *New York Times*.

Dana Shuster served in the Army Nurse Corps in Vietnam for two tours of duty from 1966 to 1968, working in the OR, ER, and ICU. She is a passionate and articulate spokesperson for the nurses of the Vietnam War. Her poems appear in *Visions of War, Dreams of Peace: Writings of Women in the Vietnam War* (Warner Books, 1991).

Kelly Sievers is a registered nurse who has specialized in anesthesia. She has poems in *Seattle Review, Poet & Critic, The Bridge, Hayden's Ferry Review, Western Journal of Medicine,* and other journals. Kelly lives in Portland, Oregon, and in 1994 received a fellowship from *Fishtrap,* an organization sponsoring conferences and workshops with an emphasis on writing and the West.

Rosemary Smith is a staff nurse on a general medical ward with twenty years of experience. "The Journey," the first piece she has published, was written to give others insight into nursing in the South Wales valleys. She has a twin brother and is the youngest of ten children brought up in a mining community in the Rhondda Valley of South Wales.

Sandra Smith is a registered nurse working in geriatric care in the Cincinnati-Dayton area. Her poetry has won awards from local and national poetry chapters, and she has coauthored a book of poetry, *Amalgam Poems* (Green Phoenix Press, 1994), with Sandra L. Elliott. Sandy also writes short stories and has a novel in progress.

Sybil Smith writes fiction and creative nonfiction. She works as a psychiatric nurse and lives with her daughter in Hartford, Vermont. Her work has appeared in *Northern Review, Vermont Woman, Albany Review, Ellipsis, Gulf Stream Magazine, Northeast Corridor, Yankee,* and other magazines and journals, and has been anthologized in *Life on the Line* (Negative Capability Press, 1992). A nonfiction account of her experience in Honduras appeared in *But Do They Have Field Experience?* (Kumarian Press, 1993).

Janet Tripp has thirty years' experience as a registered nurse in pediatrics, geriatrics, and psychiatry. She is also a writer and avid reader. Her work has appeared in *Women's Studies Quarterly, Hurricane Alice: A Feminist Quarterly,* and other regional journals, and has been anthologized in *The Book Group Book* (Chicago Review Press, 1993). She is working on a biography of Lorraine Hansberry for young adults.

Belle Waring is the author of *Refuge* (University of Pittsburgh Press, 1990), the winner of the Associated Writing Programs' Award for Poetry in 1989 and the Washington Prize in 1991. She has received fellowships from the National Endowment for the Arts, the Virginia Center for the Creative Arts, and from the Fine Arts Work Center in Provincetown, Massachusetts. She is writer-in-residence at a children's medical center in Washington, D.C. She holds degrees in nursing and English, and an M.F.A. from Vermont College.

Ellen Diderich Zimmer is a nurse educator and researcher. She has published several articles on teaching and computers in professional journals. She was a first lieutenant in the Army Nurse Corps and stationed at the 3rd Field Hospital in Saigon, Vietnam, from 1971 to 1972. She is also a freelance writer of poetry and fiction.

We are grateful to the authors who have given us permission to include previously unpublished work in this anthology. We also thank the authors, editors, and publishers who have given us permission to reprint the following selections.

Carolyn Barbier: Originally published in *Calyx: A Journal of Art and Literature by Women:* "Nighthawks." Copyright © 1994 by Carolyn Barbier. Reprinted by permission of Carolyn Barbier.

Jeanne Beall: Originally published in *Talking River Review:* "The Color of Protocol" and "Angel from Pratt Street." Copyright © 1994 and 1995 by Jeanne Beall. Reprinted by permission of Jeanne Beall.

Celia Brown: Originally published in *Federal Poet:* "Daffodil Days." Copyright © 1988 by Celia Brown. Reprinted by permission of Celia Brown. Originally published in *Salmon:* "The First Hour." Copyright © 1990 by Celia Brown. Reprinted by permission of Celia Brown. "The First Hour" also appeared in *Federal Poet* (1993).

Jeanne Bryner: Originally published in *Poetry East:* "Butterfly." Copyright © 1994 by Jeanne Bryner. Reprinted by permission of Jeanne Bryner.

Richard Callin: Originally published in *Journal of the American Medical Association:* "A Story." Copyright © 1993 by American Medical Association. Reprinted by permission of American Medical Association.

Cortney Davis: Originally published in *International Journal of Arts-Medicine:* "The Nurse's Task." Copyright © 1991 by MMB Music. Reprinted by permission of MMB Music. Originally published in *Hudson Review:* "The Body Flute." Copyright © 1994 by Cortney Davis. Reprinted by permission of Cortney Davis. Originally published in *The Body Flute*, Adastra Press: "What the Nurse Likes," "Night Nurse." Copyright © 1994 by Cortney Davis. Reprinted by permission of Cortney Davis. "The Body Flute" also appears in *The Body Flute.*

Theodore Deppe: Originally published in *Cream City Review:* "The Book of God." Copyright © 1994 by Theodore Deppe. Reprinted by permission of Theodore Deppe. Originally published in *Massachusetts Review:* "Admission, Children's Unit." Copyright © 1995 by Theodore Deppe. Reprinted by permission of Theodore Deppe. Originally published in *Children of the Air*, Alice